BY THE AUTHOR

Novels
Surviving Sting
Kiss Me Softly, Amy Turtle
Do I Love You?

Poetry
The Right Suggestion
Catch a Falling Tortoise
An Artist Goes Bananas

Criticism
Fiction from the Furnace
Student Guide to Philip Roth
Laughing at the Darkness
Reading *Catch-22*
Reading Toni Morrison's *Beloved*
Storytelling: Narratology for Critics and Creative Writers
Philip Roth Through the Lens of Kepesh
(with Samantha Roden)
The Enigmas of Confinement: A History and Poetics of Flash Fiction
Lydia Davis: A Study
Allen Ginsberg: Cosmopolitan Comic

Philosophy
The Philosophy of Humour

As Editor
Loffing Matters
The Tipping Point

DON'T USE THE PHONE

DON'T USE THE PHONE
What Poets Can Learn from Books

PAUL McDONALD

Greenwich Exchange
London

Greenwich Exchange, London

First published in Great Britain in 2023
All rights reserved

Don't Use the Phone: What Poets Can Learn from Books
© Paul McDonald, 2023

Printed and bound by imprintdigital.com
Cover design by December Publications
Tel: 07951511275

Greenwich Exchange Website: www.greenex.co.uk

Cataloguing in Publication Data is available
from the British Library

Cover: Courtesy of Shutterstock

ISBN: 978-1-910996-62-1

CONTENTS

INTRODUCTION

'People who "want to write" without being passionate about reading are digging writing's grave. You can only be as good a writer as you are a reader.'

– Ruth Padel[1]

Writers need to read. That seems very obvious, but in my years teaching creative writing to undergraduates I've been constantly astonished by people's failure to see the link between reading and writing. Poets are writers too, and this applies particularly to them. Where poets often aspire to publish a book-length collection of their poems, it's staggering how many don't take the trouble to read other people's[2]. Obviously books have a lot of competition these days, but for me smartphones pose one of the biggest threats to books, and particularly to the kind of attentive reading we associate with the page. In some ways looking at a smartphone screen is the opposite of reading, certainly with the close, critically

---

[1] Quoted in *Inside Creative Writing: Interviews with Contemporary Writers*, Graeme Harper (ed) (London: Palgrave Macmillan, 2012), 187

[2] A recent study notes that 'for under-25s [...] daily consumption of any printed material [...] declined from 60 percent in the late 1970s, to just 12 per cent in 2019', something that the authors suggest might constitute 'a crisis in reading' with a detrimental effect on people's capacity for empathy and critical acumen. Lisa Hilton, 'You Can't Make it Up' in *The Critic*, #16, April 2021, 38-40, 38/39.

engaged reading we must do if we're to be the best poets we can be: when it comes to poetry, the page is infinitely better than the screen[3]. This volume is designed to coax poets away from the clickbait mire, and return them to where they will learn most about the art of writing poetry: books. A perfect place to start is with this one.

I'll be discussing some of the most interesting poetry collections I've read in recent years, explaining what I like about them, and how I think poets can use them to improve their own writing. By poetry collections I mean the single-author slim volumes that have been the main means of poetry dissemination since Gutenberg. *Don't Use the Phone* mixes criticism with creative writing exercises and advice to show how thinking critically about poetry books can help poets develop their craft.

Don't Use the Phone

My title is adapted from a poem by the American Beat poet, Jack Kerouac:

> Don't use the telephone.
> People are never ready to answer it.
> Use poetry[4]

---

[3] There's a wealth of research on the benefits of reading books as opposed to screens. For a good survey see 'The Reading Brain in the Digital Age: The Science of Paper versus Screens' by Ferris Jabr, *Scientific American* April 11, 2013, where it's suggested that "When reading on screens, people seem less inclined to engage in what psychologists call metacognitive learning regulation – strategies such as setting specific goals, rereading difficult sections and checking how much one has understood along the way.' These strategies are key to reading and appreciating poetry.

[4] 'To Edward Dahlberg' in Gary Gach (ed) *What Book!?: Buddha Poems from Beat to Hiphop* (Berkeley: Parallax Press, 1998), 19.

For Kerouac, poetry is a superior mode of communication requiring focus and effort, and the best poets assume a degree of receptiveness, intellectual exertion, and commitment from their readers; if we're willing to give it – if we are 'ready to answer' – then the rewards can be huge. Kerouac didn't have smartphones in mind when he wrote his poem in the middle of the last century, but his words seem relevant in an age where we're preoccupied with the superficial diversions that technology promotes.

Obviously it's possible to find plenty of poetry via smartphones, but they offer unsatisfactory poetic encounters for several reasons. Firstly they take us away from poetry collections. YouTube clips, social media uploads, website samples, etc, all offer useful ways for poets to advertise, but they tend to privilege individual poems at the expense of collections.[5] Online engagement with single poems offers a different experience to the slim volume, and only in collections do we get a true feel for a poet's voice and vision: poems illuminate one another in collections, and have a cumulative effect as we read; poems in the best slim volumes have a centripetal force – they are better together. Not only do smartphones take us away from collections, they take us away from hard copy print. Our relationship with poems is more intense in *printed* books: we're inclined to concentrate harder on them, with less risk of distraction. There's a sense of permanence and materiality about hard copy books that is absent online, and a tactile, physical relationship that seems important to poetry lovers: as Simon Armitage says, books

---

[5] As Clive James noted, '[e]ven with such a literary subject as poetry, you can nowadays get a long way without taking your eyes off the computer screen, and young people in particular may scarcely encounter the traditional "slim volume" of poetry.' Clive James, *Poetry Notebook: 2006-2014* (London: Picador, 2014), 12.

'recognise the physical certainty of poetry, acknowledge the symbiotic pleasure of being possessed *by* an object while being possessor *of* it'[6]. Another important reason is that smartphones tend to favour a particular kind of poetry, notably insta and performance poetry, rather than what we might call 'page poetry'. I'm not suggesting that insta and performance poetry have no value, but such material doesn't always transcend its own language, or have a life beyond its performance context. While I wouldn't suggest that it's not 'real' poetry, much of it is geared toward the kind of immediate impact suited to a medium that reflects and feeds an accelerated and superficial culture.[7] The internet isn't the best environment for serious, intellectually engaged poetry – the kind employing complexity, subtlety, ambiguity, and demanding active rather than passive engagement. 'Page poems' feed our intellectual lives more fully, particularly when encountered in the context of a collection. As I read a slim volume I develop a feel for the voice and the mind that lies behind it, gradually becoming accustomed to that poet's perspective, aesthetic, philosophy and creative strategies – in this way their art can more readily challenge, enlighten, or provoke me into new ways of seeing, offering insights that will enhance my own creative life.

---

[6] Simon Armitage, 'When I Heard the Learn'd Astronomer' in *A Vertical Art: Oxford Lectures* (London: Faber and Faber, 2021), 299

[7] I wouldn't be as dismissive as Rebecca Watts, for instance, who caused a stir in 2018 for accusing performance and insta poetry of a 'denigration of intellectual engagement and rejection of craft' (see 'The Cult of the Noble Amateur', *PN Review*, 239, Volume 44, Number 3, January-February 2018). But I do agree that such poetry doesn't always work well on the page, and, while it can sell in huge numbers (see Rupi Kaur's best selling *Milk and Honey* (2014)), it often lacks the cerebral dimension that I personally enjoy in poetry.

How To Use This Book

I have chosen seventeen slim volumes that will be useful for developing poets to read. I've deliberately gone outside the contemporary canon to explore books that may be less familiar to general poetry readers: all of my choices come from small, independent presses. This seemed appropriate because, according to some scholars, small presses have an 'ongoing commitment to the book as a material object [...] perhaps exactly due to a fetishization of the digital in the mainstream'[8]. My own book has a similar commitment! Despite being outside the canon, my choices reflect the preoccupations of modern poetry as I see it, exploring themes like the natural world, philosophy, place, race, identity, gender, mortality, and the lived experience. I begin each discussion by citing a few complete poems from the collection, followed by a discussion of the poems and a review of the book as a whole. I also offer guidance on how we might 'use' the book as poets: ie what we can learn from it to develop our craft. Each section includes a series of writing prompts designed to facilitate deeper imaginative involvement with the texts, and an appreciation of how they might inform our own creative journey. I close each section with suggestions for further reading, again citing collections that the

---

[8] See 'Introduction: Making Publishing Visible' in *The Contemporary Small Press: Making Publishing Visible* by Georgina Colby (Editor), Kaja Marczewska (Editor), Leigh Wilson (Editor) (Palgrave Macmillan, 2021), 4. There are many different types of small, independent poetry presses, and not all of them are *that* small: some such as Bloodaxe and Carcanet are sizable publishers who, alongside mainstream publishers like Picador and Penguin, form part of the poetry establishment in the UK. I've chosen collections that come from presses existing mostly outside that establishment, whose publishing remit is less defined by commercial factors or fashion. While a couple of the presses publish titles simultaneously via ebook, all have a commitment to traditional print books, and most publish exclusively in this format.

reader may not have previously encountered. Naturally readers can use my book without reading all or any of the collections I mention – *Don't Use the Phone* works as a self-contained poetry course in its own right – but hopefully my comments will encourage further exploration of these inspiring slim volumes.

MAKING CONNECTIONS AND THE IDEA OF A COLLECTION

Given that I am advocating the importance of poetry collections, I begin by discussing a book that is relevant to the 'idea of a collection', and the significance of making connections both within and between poems. Poets and critics tend to be good at seeing connections, of course, because they are central to creativity and interpretation. Poetry collections also depend on connections: verse in slim volumes is often grouped around themes, with the relationships between individual poems offering cohesion and structure. It's with this idea in mind that I turn to the first slim volume that poets might find useful, Jo Dixon's *Purl*.

Jo Dixon's *Purl* [9]

THE ARDABIL CARPET

Expecting the downlighters
that bleed each wool-knot
on the hour on the half hour
I nudge the barrier with my shins

---

[9] Jo Dixon, *Purl* (Nottingham: Shoestring Press, 2020). All further quotations will be taken from this edition.

and lay the shape of my breath
on the display case where the flowers
tinted with pomegranate-rind
will lose another shade.

The tang of *Bisto* blends
with one more cigarette
glowing in the ashtray
and I play house on the carpet

in the front-room where Grandma
still tied into a money apron
scored with potato-soil
warms and waits for the Sunday roast.

OVERTURE

A young stag all emerging antlers
raises his nose toward a teenage couple

over by the cedar stump shrugging off its bark,
exposing boucle ridge, silky crevices
and fibrous escarpments gripped by webs.

On the next bench
moisture in wooden slats soaks their jeans
and a plaque reassures *Pleasure and Companionship*
                    Found Here
while he defines her shoulder blade with his fingertips

and toes the browned pine needles pulped in the mud
like wedding rice on a wet day
                    If you want to be in a relationship-

Later he steers her around the Camellia House
rainwater performing on glazed roof-lights
and petals warping on stone flags

her eyes downcast, tracing the entangled circles of bronze grilles
above heating ducts where pennies have been lost.

NICU

I
buzzed in at nine

through the porthole
a boy with wrinkle-sag
knees shelters his fingers
in the antiseptic furrows
of your cupped palm;
from your perch
on next door's vacant
stool, you anticipate
back spasms

four hours later
litmus paper stutters
in your fingers – *is pink
red?* and your milk tubes
down into his stomach

now a sodden slippery nappy sags
on the cannula impaled
in his gauzy vein; cotton
wool and titanium ointment
jumble around his legs

at bedtime
your lullaby keeps time

with his heart's
beep

buzzed out at nine.

II
It's just in case.
A Polaroid, 23 by 3 1\2" :
tangles of tubes and wires snake to a body frozen
in the position of his foetal scan
air pushes down the endotracheal tube and he breathes
the right pattern.

Tuck him under your pillow.

My Weaving Grants Me Sight: Reading Jo Dixon's *Purl*

Jo Dixon apparently discovered the theme for this book as she
assembled her poems for publication: in one interview she claims
to have found the various meanings of the word 'purl' 'resonating
with all the poems' *after* they were written, suggesting the extent
to which the unconscious is at work when poets write: what she
initially assumed were discrete poems had connections she missed
until she began to reflect on them[10]. The book splits into three
sections, corresponding with the three principal meanings of the
word 'purl': firstly, and perhaps most commonly, as used in
knitting; secondly as a verb meaning 'to flow with a swirling motion'
[21]; thirdly as a colloquial term for overturning, or tipping 'head
over heels' [35].

---

[10] *Poetry from Maria Taylor and Jo Dixon* (Five Leaves Bookshop online event
recording)

The opening poem of Section I is 'The Ardabil Carpet', included above. It pursues the idea of weaving, both literally and figuratively: it links a memory of the speaker having once seen the famous Ardabil Carpet 'in a display case', with a memory of playing on a carpet as a child while her grandma 'warms and waits for the Sunday roast' [3]. Notice how the two main images gain significance in juxtaposition – a connection between unrelated carpets generates a memory of childhood, although we don't know precisely how to read this; she mentions that the 'flowers' in the old Persian carpet are fading, and there are potential parallels between this and her grandmother's aging, and maybe her own, but we can't say much more than this. However, our not knowing doesn't make it a bad poem – the juxtaposition creates an intriguing atmosphere, rather than making a direct statement, hinting at the inevitability of decline, perhaps, or the oddness of felt associations. It presents images for the reader to knit (purl) together, with a minimal amount of contextualisation from the poet. The onus is on us to make sense of the connections, to weave them together like a carpet. In this way the poem forces us to make a creative investment: we have to think like a poet, linking images and ideas in order to *make* them meaningful. Whenever a poem feels odd or obscure, a good tip is to try and imagine that you have written it yourself, and to consider what *you* might have meant by it. For me the poem is *about* connections, the carpet imagery connecting (weaving) past and present across generations and history, albeit in a mysterious, ultimately inexplicable way.

Dixon's poems often work through an accumulation of disparate images, as with 'Overture', where she seems to present the beginning of a romance. The scene appears to be a park or public garden – 'A young stag' is glimpsed in the opening stanza, 'raising his nose toward a teenage couple' – and from there on we're presented with selected close descriptions of their immediate surroundings, from 'the cedar stump shrugging off its bark' to the wet 'wooden slats' of the bench on which they sit [5]. It exemplifies William Carlos Williams's dictum, 'No ideas but in things'[11], presenting an incipient relationship in the form of images and impressions without explaining them, inviting us to infer their significance. The poem closes with the couple having entered the Camellia House, but it's hard to say what the reference to her 'downcast' distraction means, not to mention the lost pennies: how should we read these against the opening image of the young stag? We have little to guide us, other than our innate inclination to seek significance in 'things': to 'purl' them together, or find the 'purl' that binds them. Again, rather than make meaning explicit, it creates a mood: the vigour and promise of the young stag is implicitly qualified by the downcast eyes and the reference to loss, perhaps suggesting that the couple should have tempered their expectations, and implying that readers do the same. The creative engagement it demands from us makes us active readers, and there's much satisfaction to be had from making the connections Dixon's images invite, and reflecting on their significance. I don't know her intentions, or whether she has a single meaning in mind, and I don't need to: part of the joy is *not* knowing, something we'd be denied if the connections were made explicit.

---

[11] It is a line from the 1927 version of his epic poem, *Paterson*. As a concept it became associated with Imagism, with its emphasis on the direct focus on concrete images.

I haven't included any complete poems from Section II of *Purl* here, but they mostly address the idea of 'purl' in relation to movement, whether it's the waltzers in a poem called 'Market Garden Way, National Memorial Arboretum', where 'clasped hands tingle and trap the warmth' as they dance [26], or 'the trajectory/ of a palm-blown kiss' in 'Collecting Evidence' [32], which is another lovely poem from this book. Sometimes the flow ('purl') in this section relates to water or birds, as with the 'slow flowing river' in 'To the Fates', where a bird skims the surface with 'lightning-blue mantle nape to tail'; in this poem it's the speaker's 'weaving' eye that allows her to see and appreciate the elusive bird, as she learns to align herself to the 'purl' of the natural world: 'my weaving/ grants me sight' [23], we're told in the final line.

It's not always possible to move smoothly with the flow of life, and Section III deals with the colloquial meaning of 'purl' in relation to mishaps, accidents, and worlds upended. Several poems not included in my sample allude to war: there's an unexploded bomb in 'South Bank Catch Up', for instance, which is 'towed out past Essex, detonated' as friends 'catch up' at a riverside restaurant, and we're left wondering about the dark implications of the historical ordinance as a symbol of ever-present danger [52]. Another war poem, 'Variations on a Theme, 1943' offers a tribute to the lighthouse keepers killed in WWII [51]. Most of the poems in this section reference life's vicissitudes, then, and not surprisingly some are set in hospitals, including the one I've included above, 'NICU'. This describes visiting a premature baby in a Neonatal Intensive Care Unit. Part I presents a series of sense impressions of a parent's daily vigil, observing 'a boy with wrinkle-sag/knees'

[53]. The poem closes with a shorter second part, and a reference to a Polaroid taken of the baby. The sections are separated by time – part I describes the mother's visit, part II refers to a period in the evening when the mother is alone. The connections are more obvious than in some of the other poems, and the ending is unusual for its explanatory opening line: we're told that the Polaroid has been taken 'just in case' – in other words so that the mother will have something to remember the baby by 'just in case' he dies. This is poignant in itself, but it's given more force by the broader context of the collection, and the idea of 'purl' that has been established throughout the final section: the poem acknowledges the ever-present threat of the colloquial 'purl' of mishap and disaster, together with a very human need to protect against it; the Polaroid represents an attempt to assert control and agency in a world of chaos and contingency, and we feel this more strongly if we make connections with the poems that precede it. In other words, while 'NICU' is touching and beautiful as a stand-alone poem, it's even better in the book because the previous poems augment our understanding of its themes and facilitate a more emotionally nuanced and intense engagement.

Writing poems is a creative act, but finding connections between them is an imaginative and edifying enterprise in its own right. As well as inviting us to make connections within poems, Dixon makes connections between the poems: indeed, it's the connections that make this book a book. When read as a collection, rather than as a series of disparate poems, *Purl* builds into a book partly *about* connections, and about making meaning: ultimately we 'purl' each meaning of 'purl' together, and find our experience of life reflected:

the creative purl, the purl of movement, and the purl of unpredictability, all of which seem fundamental to our experience of the world. This idea is implied rather than stated: indeed, to state it in such a reductive way makes it sound strained and implausible, but I sense these associations as I read the book, expressed with a subtlety that's peculiar to poetry. Now it's almost as if the word 'purl' has a fourth, poetry-related meaning for me that it would not have without Dixon's book.

How Can Poets Use It?

• As poets we can learn from Dixon's skill at creating meaningful juxtapositions: she is adept at presenting images and ideas in ways that invite us to connect and interpret them, reminding us perhaps of the relationship between poetry and criticism: both activities involve drawing significance from the world as we perceive it, building meaning from the patterns and connections we discern; some juxtapositions seem more meaningful than others, of course, and the poet's job, like the critic's, is to spot the most meaningful of all.

• Poets can also learn a lot from how Dixon structures *Purl*: the insightful way in which she groups poems in her collection reveals another aspect of her ability to make meaningful associations: in this way she creates an integrated collection, adding amplitude and layers of meaning to her writing.

• Dixon lets her images speak for themselves: in keeping with William Carlos Williams's advice, her ideas are mainly in 'things', and her emphasis is on showing rather than telling.

Writing Prompts

• Think of some strong images from childhood, as Dixon does in 'The Ardabil Carpet', and then think of some more images from the here and now: the childhood images might be clothes, favourite possessions, holidays, etc; the here and now should be adult images of the same things (eg *current* clothes, possessions, holidays, etc). Describe each as faithfully as possible, and with as much detail as you can muster. Once you have a list from past and present, spend some time comparing: does any image resonate with another, the way Dixon's do in 'The Ardabil Carpet'? Put the best two together in the form of a poem, trying to resist the temptation to explain any significance you discern: remember to show it rather than tell it.

• Select a word from the dictionary that has several meanings (like 'purl') and write poems reflecting or responding to each different definition of the word. This exercise can sometimes add an interesting new dimension to the chosen word as the poems combine to suggest previously undetected connections.

Slim Volumes in a Similar Vein

If you enjoyed *Purl* you might also enjoy *Ai! Ai! Pianissimo* by Astrid Alben (Arc Publications, 2011), *The Plate Spinner* by Denise

McSheehy (Oversteps Books, 2017), *In the Curator's Hands* by Abegail Morley (Indigo Dreams, 2017), *How to Grow Matches* by S.A. Leavesley (Against the Grain Poetry Press, 2018), *Footnotes to Water* by Zoë Skoulding (Seren, 2019), and *Yield* by Claire Dyer (Two Rivers Press, 2021).

MYSTERIOUS NATURE I: THE NON-HUMAN

Ecological issues have become increasingly important for artists and thinkers in the twenty-first century, and poets have inevitably searched for ways of positioning themselves within environmental debates. The term 'ecopoetry' has much currency, and is often used to categorize poetry that, in Jonathan Bate's words, 'is not a description of dwelling with the earth, not a disengaged thinking about it, but an experiencing of it'[12]. We can see this in the work of numerous high profile poets: in books like *Dart* (2007), for instance, Alice Oswald challenges Romantic notions of landscape as 'picturesque', finding ways of decentering the human ego in our encounters with nature, offering non-judgemental representations of the non-human world. Similarly, one of John Burnside's key themes as a poet has been exploring ways of living sympathetically, avoiding tendencies toward the exploitation and domination of nature[13]. Modern ecopoetry often dwells on the strangeness and unfathomable qualities of nature, respecting its status as an enigma. While the work of writers like Oswald and Burnside is justly

---

[12] Jonathan Bate, *The Song of the Earth* (London: Picador, 2001), 42

[13] For a discussion see Borthwick, D. 'The sustainable male: masculine ecology in the poetry of John Burnside'. In *Masculinity and the Other: Historical Perspectives* (Cambridge Scholars Publishing, Newcastle upon Tyne, 2009), 63-85

celebrated, there are many lesser known ecopoets whose work deserves attention: in this section I'll discuss two of them.

Anna Selby's *Field Notes*[14]

SEA CUCUMBERS

Holothuria forskali
I go to the sea when I'm lousy with sleep
startled, half-dreaming, beneath
one-part waking to three-parts deep.
Tonight, I walk down to the harbour
past the catcalls, the men, the neon takeaways
great thighs of kebab meat pivot in lit windows.
I push my body down into the water
to hide under the cuff of the waves
lying, arms folded
watching fish turn their silver.
I am their inmate:
drifting over them as we roll. We blow
and are a kiss blown back.
Through a blur of spit in my goggles
I study leopard-dotted sea cucumbers
fat, thick, huge as porno cocks in the greasy water.
I see one pour itself into a rock
observing this beautiful punk
unchaining its skin
liquefying. When I surface, the men
lean over the harbour wall.
I recall a film I saw on the telly
accidentally when I was eight
where a woman gets gang-raped

---

[14] Anna Selby, *Field Notes* (Sandy: Hazel Press Publishers, 2020). All quotations will be taken from this edition.

on a pin-ball machine.
The harbour men
flick their cigarettes, staring
starting down the steps.
Disco lights pucker, slip.
Everything is inconsistent.

LOS ABRIGOS I

To follow fish under water is to be a giant, inviting
herself to a waltz; waltzing alone. The underneath
waves rolling through rocks, when the waters'
catch on the thing they touch. Jumping from rocks
into the sea. To jump is to bullet. Burn the water.

It's hard to write in here without getting wet!

Was it there? Tiger shark. Does it scare me that it
isn't there now? Underwater disorientation.

Trumpettish. The letter-opener fish. Two fish put
together. Long and thin. Mr Tickle. Cartoon
character. Made up. A child invented you. Jazz solo.
Alone always – at first. I think it's a loose bit of
seaweed. Stray. Drifting.

Families of wrasse. Damselfish, all different sizes.
The sand tiger looked prehistoric and unhelpful.
Pipefish.

Trumpetfish. *Aulostomus strigosus.* Half my height. Elusive.
Party drifter. Frills. Crab-orange. Salmon eye.
Fascinating. I could follow you endlessly through
these rocks.

Ornate Wrasse family. Seeing others off. Dogs.
Territorial. Chromatophores

WHAT HAPPENS TO YOUR HEART

It goes like this:
you will be floating
your skin will become thirst.
Submerge your face
a metamorphosis starts
blood retreats, heartbeat slowing
your mind an almost-state.
If you choose
dive, the transformation
grows. You become water
mammalian. On land
the equivalent pressure
kills. For the first few feet
your lungs are buoys, afterwards
contracting air shrinks you.
go deeper, you swim
into a gravityless space
here is where the ocean
stops pushing you away
further, the pressure trebles
the Master Switch kicks, your heart
ticks even slower, below
it plummets – 14 beats
or lower, you should be unconscious
your chest size halves, organ walls
work as release valves.
Now, turn back up.
Everything switches
re-inflates, races.

You are land again, of and on.
Your heart broke laws.

You Become Water: Reading Anna Selby's *Field Notes*

Anna Selby's collection *Field Notes* (2020) is published by Hazel Press, a tiny publisher with a particular interest in environmental themes. It begins with a quote from Joan Didion about otherness and difference between genders:

> what it is like to be a woman,
> the irreconcilable difference of it –
> that sense of living one's deepest life
> underwater, that dark involvement
> with blood and birth and death [5]

As we read *Field Notes* we find that the notion of 'difference' and 'involvement' extends beyond what it's 'like to be a woman', to the relationship between the human and the non-human. Selby acknowledges the 'irreconcilable difference' between the former and the latter: while the non-human is unknowable, she senses a 'dark involvement' with it, stressing her link to nature and the interrelatedness of self and other. Selby's method as a poet is interesting: she aims for artistic immersion in a literal sense, and many of the notes on which the poems are based were actually written under water, which she feels gives her work more 'immediacy, and intimacy', helping her to the avoid the 'anthropomorphism that can pollute our relationships with creatures'[15].

Several poems are about the ways in which we get nature wrong;

---

[15] See the poet's website at http://www.annamariaselby.co.uk/poetry.html

in 'Sea Cucumbers' the speaker is uncomfortable in what she sees as a world of sexual objectification, and she seeks solace in the sea, walking 'down to the harbour past the catcalls, the men' [9]. The speaker is fleetingly transported by nature, feeling in harmony with it: she can hide 'under the cuff' of the waves, drifting in sync with the roll of the ocean. Nature is briefly anthropomorphised and idealised as she and the sea become like lovers, blowing kisses to one another; but the tone shifts again as the poem develops, and the fact that sea cucumbers remind her of 'porno cocks' reveals how she views nature through the lens of ideology: she cannot help but invoke the language and imagery that she's inherited from patriarchy, and which shapes her thinking. There's no escape from it. As soon as she re-enters the social realm the sexual threat returns: she is sexualised by the leering harbour men, just as *she* has sexualised the sea cucumber. It implies that the meaning of nature is partly dependent on ideology: it is socially derived, and as long as this is the case '[e]verything' will remain 'inconsistent', because ideology is constantly in flux. Nature's *real* meaning remains elusive – we can only understand it in relation to our cultural narratives and social conditioning, which in this case means making cocks out of cucumbers!

The idea of nature as unknowable registers often in the book, and is sometimes evident at the level of form. Notice how the underwater world becomes increasingly strange in 'Los Abrigos I': at first being in the water is like 'inviting/herself to a waltz; waltzing alone' [22], but as the poem progresses, the encounter with nature becomes a more complicated dance, much harder to fathom in human terms, until it fails to resemble a dance at all. In the final stanzas language breaks down as the world gets weirder, and the speaker struggles to make it cohere: what begins as structured narrative becomes increasingly fragmented, a series of sense impressions that refuse to be fully integrated – the staccato effect reflects the buffeting of the sea. It ends with a single word sentence, 'Chromatophores': in other words, after a series of images evoking colour, she closes with the word for a type of cell that *makes* colour, almost as if she gives up on description, leaving nature to speak for itself. As the world gradually breaks down into its constituent parts, we're left only with cryptic impressions.

At the same time, of course, we are inextricably connected to nature, which is a point made in 'What Happens to Your Heart'. This poem is about the effects that the sea has on the body when we are submerged. As we go deeper, pressure increases and bodies respond accordingly: 'blood retreats, heartbeat slowing' until 'You become water' [10]. It's concerned with how we are connected to, and influenced by, the natural world, subject to its processes: when we are submerged in water we 'become' it, reminding us that, in a manner of speaking, we *are* it. The poem's final line 'Your heart broke laws' reminds us that we are inextricably bound to nature, and when we break its laws we break our own: humanity is a manifestation of the natural world, and not separate from it; when we mistreat it it's a personal violation.

How Can Poets Use It?

> • Selby's book offers a wonderful example of a poet striving
> to create immersive verse. This is clear from her method,
> which involves taking notes whilst *literally* immersed in

water. Her method and style impacts both on the force of her imagery and the texture of her descriptive detail, but it also registers in the rhythms of her language, as seen in 'Los Abrigos I', and very often elsewhere in the book. Before we write about nature we could do worse than to study this, and the sense of physicality she manages to capture as a result of her willingness to engage directly with her subject.

• Like Dixon, Selby is a good example of a poet who lets images speak for themselves; this is particularly important when writing about nature, where any attempts to explain or resolve its otherness can easily feel reductive and self-serving.

• Notice how she uses lineation and staccato phrasing to create atmosphere and drama in poems like 'Los Abrigos I': the word 'Pipefish' is a single-word stanza, followed by a longer, fragmented stanza that presents words and phrases without connectives; this is an example of parataxis, reflecting a rapid sequence of impressions without privileging a single one, other than the Pipefish itself.

Writing Prompts

• Read 'Sea Cucumbers' and write a poem from the point of view of a fish being observed by a snorkeler. Pretend that you can read the snorkeler's mind, then list all the things the snorkeler gets wrong about you. Is it possible to find ways of legitimising your need to anthropomorphise the fish?

• Read 'Los Abrigos I' and write a poem about being under water, trying to capture the feel of the water, the buffeting of the currents, and how the different environment impacts on you physically and emotionally.

• Read 'What Happens to Your Heart' and imagine that you have a desire to drink the entire ocean in order to be at one with it. How would you describe such an impossible and self-destructive thirst?

Slim Volumes in a Similar Vein

If you like *Field Notes* you might also enjoy *Lightyear* by Alison Fell (Smokestack, 2005), *ECOZOA* by Helen Moore (Permanent Publications, 2015), *Fossil* by Maya Chowdhry (Peepal Tree Press, 2016), *Words the Turtle Taught Me* by Susan Richardson (Cinnamon Press, 2018), *Raven Mothers* by Breda Wall Ryan (Doire Press, 2018), *This Tilting Earth* by Jane Lovell (Seren, 2019), *Life Without Air* by Daisy Lafarge (Granta Books, 2020), and *What is Near* by Kay Syrad (Cinnamon Press, 2021).

Ian Marriott's *The Hollow Bone*[16]

THE WILD
Careful and deadly,
the wolf pack
dead-woods
its native elk –

---

[16] Ian Marriott, *The Hollow Bone* (Blaenau Ffestiniog: Cinnamon Press, 2017). All quotations will be taken from this edition.

gardener snipping
captive roses –
great white secateurs
prune hard back.

*

It is a fact
that the wild
and the tame
do not mix.

Fox in its hen-house
drunk on hens –
wolf amok
in a ranchers yard –

a deer high-tailing
the strangeness of sheep –
or the mind writhing
in its sack of sleep

THE MIGRATION OF CARIBOU

And what of the caribou
on their northern slope –
born to run beside the mother
as her mother before.

Each spring
a river of knowing –
flooding the tundra,
the cotton grass slopes,

until in the end
it's all there is –
this hunger for elsewhere,
the birthing grounds,

forgotten completely
the skin she was born to –
a woman swimming
to reach her own bank.

STRANGE

At low tide
inking across the limpid pool
I thought I'd taken your measure,

but years later we met again
and nothing could have been
further from the truth –

with your parrot's beak
and eight-legged intelligence
morphing through

that rusted port-hole
so impossibly
smaller than yourself.

And it wasn't the fact
that you'd done it at all,
but the way

you'd gone about the task –
I put it somewhere between

magician and master craftsman,

slowly turning
through the Rubik of your body –
until, with the flick of a wrist

you're through –
gathering together on the other side,
this place too strange to fathom.

This Place Too Strange to Fathom: Reading Ian Marriott's *The Hollow Bone*

Similar enthusiasm for the natural world can be seen in Ian Marriott's first full collection, *The Hollow Bone* (2017), which won a Cinnamon Press Debut Collection Award, judged by the ecopoet Susan Richardson. Like Selby, he insists on nature's unknowable otherness, often standing in awe of its mystery and extremity, whilst at the same time respecting our connection to it. In 'The Wild', for instance, he reminds us that 'wild' and 'tame' is an artificial distinction created by humans; he reveals how the wild perpetually encroaches on the tame: references like 'fox in the hen house' and 'wolf amok' [55] conjure the unsettling aspects of the wild that we strive to repress – the unyielding and frightening energies of the natural world which won't be contained, and which re-emerge in our nightmares. The final stanza links nature to a dreamlife, underscored with phrases like 'strangeness of sheep' and 'sack of sleep', the half-rhyme skillfully binding the language.

In *The Hollow Bone* there is often a threat of nature reclaiming us, as can be seen in several of the poems that I don't have room to include in full here. 'The Cathedrals are Sinking', for instance, is about how the non-human is set to overrun the sinking Winchester Cathedral. Despite our best efforts to preserve this tribute to our God, it appears inevitable that the 'goddess' of nature will have her way, as the closing stanza makes clear:

> shunned goddess
> of cave and fen
> reclaiming – without malice –
> what was hers
> all along. [58]

The 'goddess/of cave and fen' – the inviolable forces of the natural world – will not be ignored, and we cannot help but feel that Marriott is delighted by this notion! But where is the 'goddess', and what motivates her – what are the forces that animate nature? He tries to find metaphors for these unanswerable questions in poems like 'The Migration of Caribou', cited in full above. Here we're told that a caribou is 'born to run beside the mother/as her mother before', and their compulsion to migrate is likened to 'a woman swimming/to reach her own bank' [27]. This metaphor suggests that the goal and the self are one: in likening a caribou to a woman he is implying that, while such drives are unknowable, they are also fundamental and pervasive throughout nature, reinforcing the connection between human and non-human.

Marriott's love for nature's ineffable, sublime forces can be seen particularly in 'Strange', a superb poem about the sheer weirdness of an octopus. Notice how initially the speaker feels that he understands the creature: he says 'I thought I'd taken your measure', but, as with Anna Selby, he comes to see that it's never quite possible to take the 'measure' of anything in the non-human world. Later, when he sees the creature force its way through a hole 'so impossibly/smaller than yourself', he can only marvel at its oddness and otherness as it gathers 'together on the other side' [54]. Again this poem alludes to all that lies beyond the knowable human world as the creature seems to defy the laws of nature – it suggests a world that can't be fully conceptualised in human terms. Marriott's flair for imagery is such that he helps us feel its weirdness, and share his joy at these enigmas. The image of 'the Rubik of your body', together with the phrase 'flick of the wrist', for instance, link three things: the idea of the octopus as a baffling puzzle, the action of a human trying to solve it, and the movement of a tentacle through water. It's an effective vehicle for Marriott's sense of wonder, which in turn stimulates our own, and our pleasure in a writer who renders the natural world with such flair, sensitivity, and respect.

How Can Poets Use It?

• Marriott's lean, precise language offers a useful model for poets: his aesthetic is underpinned by economy, and a strong awareness of lineation; note how his short lines slow down the reading process in poems like 'Wild', throwing his language and images into relief, inviting us to savour them.

• Marriott is a startlingly visual poet who clearly spends time developing his imagery, and poets should note how effective this is in poems like 'Strange'. At times his imagery is reminiscent of the defamiliarizing comparisons associated with the Martian School of poets, such as Craig Raine and Christopher Reid, who put overt, eccentric imagery at the heart of their aesthetic.[17]

• Like most good poets, Marriott is very aware of the musicality of language; while he rarely uses full rhymes, he employs assonance to wonderful effect, occasionally reinforcing it with subtle alliteration, as in phrases like 'magician and master craftsman' in the poem 'Strange'. It works because it doesn't feel forced, and poets should study his adept use of timbre and cadence, and the effective way it functions within his short line free verse.

• Like Selby, he writes about the natural world in a sensitive and informed way, eschewing naivety and sentimentality, always unwilling to impose reductive meanings on nature.

Writing Prompts

• Read 'The Wild', and imagine waking up in the night to find a wild animal in the room. Pick an animal that you fear: describe its smell, perhaps, and the noises that it makes in the dark that have alerted you to its presence. Do you dare switch the light on? Describe the debate you have with yourself about the wisdom of this, and what might happen if you decide to flick the switch!

---

[17] For a discussion of Martianism see, for instance, Sean O'Brien's *The Deregulated Muse: Essays on Contemporary British and Irish Poetry* (Bloodaxe, 1998), or Alan Robinson's *Instabilities in Contemporary British Poetry* (Macmillan, 1988)

• Read 'The Migration of Caribou', and think about how Marriott uses metaphor. Try to create a comparison from nature to describe your relationship with a family member, and the emotions they evoke.

• Read 'Strange' and then write a detailed description of the oddest animal you can think of. Like Marriott, try to find striking images that foreground the mystery of the creature, and make your inability to know it (and hence own or control it) the point of the poem.

Slim Volumes in a Similar Vein

If you enjoy *The Hollow Bone* you might also like *What They Say in Avenale* by Caroline Maldonado (Indigo Dreams, 2016), *The Tongues of Earth* by Mark Abley (Coteau Books, 2016), *Imperatives* by Pat Farrington (Lapwing Press, 2017), and *Stranger* by David Punter (Cinnamon Press, 2020).

MYSTERIOUS NATURE II: THE HUMAN

Poets like Selby and Marriott are inspired by the mysteries of nature, then, and they are at pains to stress our connection to the natural world. Now I'll turn from the non-human to the human, and explore two poets who address mysterious nature in a different way: the first in terms of human biology, the second in terms of our emotional relationships with, and within, the natural world.

---

[18] Alison Calder, *Connectomics: Poems of the Brain* (Cullercoats: Iron Press, 2017). All quotations will be taken from this edition.

Alison Calder's *Connectomics: Poems of the Brain*[18]

CONNECTOMICS

The idea is
to render the brain
transparent enough to read through,
like trickles of water washing away thought.

Deletions, insertions, translocations, inversions,
proofreaders' symbols carve a straight line
to the minotaur.

In the light of the laboratory,
thought's skein unravels,
bumpy road smoothing.

Lucent, pellucid, the brain wavers
like the glass in a display case,
minimum interference between eye and page.

Like reading through a jellyfish.
The text, however, remains opaque.

CHIMERA

Autoclave heats,
mousetakes cartograft.
Mark this: in *neuvo*science, it's genedict,
indentifraction packed in a spiral suitcase.
Nouveau-logist, embroidering,
noodling with needles, nuclear
witch graft. New pattern
humonetized:
A N D.

CHIMERA 2

When one-eyed Polyphemus asks Odysseus his name,
he answers *no man*,
the original 'who's on first?'

Trapped in the cave, Odysseus
Speaks monstrously. He is not himself.

To get out of the hole,
he grabs an animal, hangs on.
Polyphemus, groping at the cave's mouth,
feels only beast:
No man has blinded me.

The One Inside the One That Looks Like You: Reading Alison Calder's *Connectomics*

Like most poetry lovers I am interested in language, and I particularly enjoy poetry that employs language from unexpected registers. *Connectomics* by Alison Calder, uses the language of neuroscience, which struck me as brave when I first encountered it, and infinitely fascinating the more I engaged with Calder's curious book. Calder is an English-born poet who was raised in Canada, and *Connectomics* was her first UK collection, published by the North Shields based Iron Press in 2017. It's a short book, gorgeously decorated with illustrations of brains and brain cells. It includes an introduction by the philosopher and neuroscientist, Raymond Tallis, who adds context and scientific weight to Calder's poems, deeming the collection 'a dialogue [...] between the language of neuroscience, and that of imagination' [8]. Most of the poems' titles are neuroscience related, each taking a term or concept and exploring it, letting the 'dialogue' between science and the imagination develop. We're helped a little as readers by the fact that Calder includes informal and accessible footnotes explaining the terminology. We learn, for instance, that 'Roughly speaking, the goal of connectomics is to improve ways to map the neural connections in the brain' [11]. Notice the phrase 'Roughly speaking', and her use of the word 'improve' rather than 'perfect': it's the careful language of someone with an acute awareness of the brain as an enigma, and an apparent conviction that it is likely to remain one.

In the book's title poem, 'Connectomics', she makes the objective of connectomics clear, but at the same time suggests that, when it comes to the brain and the mind, clarity is achieved only fleetingly, if at all. Thus the reference to transparency in the third line is immediately qualified by a reference to transience ('trickles of water washing away thought'); the poem implies that knowledge is always likely to remain frustratingly elusive, closing with a stanza that reinforces this point: it's 'Like reading through a jellyfish', we're told, and hence language always 'remains opaque' [11]. The poem uses the strangeness of the natural world to augment our sense of our own strangeness: it's the mystery of the brain that attracts Calder, then, and it's this that makes it an ideal subject for poetry.

One of the many enjoyable things about Connectomics is how well the language of neuroscience lends itself to poetry; the terminology is powerful and poetic in itself: she has poems with titles like 'Glia', for instance, referring to 'the cells that provide support to the neurons' [24], and 'Synaptic Cleft', which is 'the small gap between two neurons, across which information passes'

[31]. Of course Calder brings her own imagination and lyricism to bear on these concepts too, unpacking them in ways which explicate them beautifully. In one of the poems that I haven't included in full here, 'Flattened Cortex', a brain is compared to 'A grand piano dropped from a window'; it ends with the following lines:

> Metaphors unstack: the poem
> is an ocean inside out. How now
> describe the nesting doll,
> the one inside the one that looks like you? [36]

Has there ever been a better description of the Tardis-like nature of the brain than 'an ocean inside out'? While Calder constantly reminds us that this and all descriptions are inadequate, the implication is that poets come closer to the truth (or a truth) than scientists – the only way you can know the brain is via the subjective experience of having one, and this presents a problem for science, with its emphasis on objectivity and empiricism: such a subjective business is better suited to poetry, which, unlike science, has the capacity to turn oceans 'inside out', metaphorically at least. Thus in this poem we are reminded that it's human beings who are the subject of the neuroscientists' investigation – the 'nesting doll' at the heart of the investigation is *us* – and this fact alone necessitates a discourse more comfortable with subjectivity than certainty.

The language of neuroscience itself references the unknowable, as we learn elsewhere in the book. For instance, neuroscience uses the term 'chimera' to refer to combinations of 'DNA from two or more separate fertilized zygotes'; but Calder reminds us that the word 'chimera' also refers to 'a monster made up of a goat, a lion, and a serpent', *and* to 'something that is impossible and cannot exist' [42-43]. Language is slippery, in other words, just like the results of neuroscience research. I have included Calder's two short poems about brain 'chimera' above, both of which respond to its weirdness and apparent impossibility. In the first, titled simply 'Chimera', she splices disparate words together to reflect the genetic recombination associated with the 'chimera' of brain chemistry: the new combinations hint at meaning – 'spiral suitcase', for instance, suggests the three dimensional spiral of DNA, while the term 'witch graft' links skin grafting to dark magic, stressing the occult dimension of this esoteric science, about which so much remains unknown. We struggle to find meaning in this fragmented poem, and it is fitting that the final capitalised conjunctive, 'A N D', leads nowhere. This emulates the experience of brain research, which always seems to lead to deeper enigmas, requiring yet another explanation to make sense of the last: neuroscience always seems to end with an 'and … ?'

She explores 'chimera' in a different way in 'Chimera 2', where she invokes Greek mythology. Calder returns us to one of the oldest jokes in literature: the pun on the phrase 'no man' that tricks the Cyclops, Polyphemus, into letting Odysseus escape the cave in Homer's epic, *The Odyssey*. The line 'feels only beast' [44] references Polyphemus's myopia in missing the human that lies beneath the meat when his prisoners escape in fleeces; the implication is that neuroscientists also risk missing something important if they limit their study of the brain to chemistry alone. Like Polyphemus, brain surgeons are easily fooled, operating in the dark as the truth escapes, disguised in this case as 'no man' or something 'that cannot exist'. Calder's point, as always, is that science isn't enough to understand such mysteries: we need poetry too.[19]

How Can Poets Use It?

• I would recommend studying Calder's inventive use of language, particularly the ostensibly incongruous discourse of science. She brings her creative imagination to bear on language, using uncommon words and concepts as a springboard into new territory, testing the boundaries of meaning and creating fresh ideas and connections. Despite the fact that her writing is grounded in a serious scientific subject, we have a strong sense of a poet at play, which for me adds an engaging energy to her work.

• Calder is also aware of the narratives she has inherited as a poet (see the references to Greek mythology), and she finds ways of weaving them into her work in the form of substructure and allusion (see particularly 'Chimera 2'). This gives allusive weight to her writing, and also offers a context within which abstruse ideas can be unpacked and interrogated, and of course understood in different ways.

Writing Prompts

• Read the poem 'Connectomics', and then pick a medical

---

[19] Many scientists believe that poetry and science have a complementary relationship. Those interested in exploring this notion might look at *A Sonnet to Science: Scientists and their Poetry* by Sam Illingworth (Manchester University Press, 2019).

procedure on any part of the human body (for instance, heart bypass, kidney cyst removal, plastic surgery). Research the procedure and familiarise yourself with the appropriate scientific terminology, then describe the surgery in the form of a poem.

• Read 'Chimera' and collect some technical jargon associated with any organ of the human body. Pick the weirdest words and then try to imagine some alternative definitions for them.

• Read 'Chimera 2' and think of a non-human character from a myth or fairy story: write a poem in which that character tries to steal your brain. Why do they want a human brain?

Slim Volumes in a Similar Vein

If you enjoy *Connectomics* you might also like *Element* by Rachel McCarthy (Smith/doorstop, 2015), *Standard Candles* by Alice Major (University of Alberta Press, 2016), *Edge* by Katrina Porteous (Bloodaxe, 2019), *Mock Orange* by Anne Osbourn (SPM Publications, 2020), and *Litany of a Cardiologist* by Denise Bundred (Against the Grain Poetry Press, 2020).

---

[20] Jo Bell, *Kith* (Rugby: Nine Arches Press, 2015). All quotations will be taken from this edition.

Jo Bell's *Kith*[20]

CRATES

Observe that when I speak of crates
your mind supplies one straight away.

Likely you are thinking of the fruiterer's crate:
a shallow slatted box of rain-napped pine,
the archetype of apples stencilled on the side,
a cartouche slot above it for a grocer's hand.

Your crate may be the sturdy plastic tub
of the eco-minded council, waiting at the gate
with all its rinsed tomato cans
and in this case a drowned frog;

or then again the solid, beer-smoothed wood
hefted by the publican
with its hungover slump of bottles
to the yard, the morning after.

Your crate exists as soon as it is thought.
Its shape is shown in speaking of it.
Now, let us speak of love.

LIFTED

The land says – *come uphill*: and water says
I will. But take it slow.

A workman's ask and nothing fancy –
Will you? Here's an answer, engineered.

A leisurely machine, a box of oak and stone;
the mitred lock, the water's *YES.*

We're stopped. The bow bumps softly
at the bottom gate, and drifts.

All water wants, all water ever wants,
is to fall. So, we use the fall to lift us,

make of water its own tool, as simple
as a crowbar or a well-tied knot;

open up the paddles, let it dam and pucker,
lift and with it, lift us like a bride, a kite,

a wanted answer, breath no longer held
or like a boat. We're on our way

and rising. Water rushes in like fools;
these tonnages that slip across the cill,

all dirty-bottle green and gathering into
a giddy hurl then slower, slow until

it ends in glassy bulges, hints of aftermath:
a cool and thorough spending.

Wait, then, for the shudder in the gate,
the backward-drifting boat that tells you

there and here are equal, an imbalance
righted. Ask of it – water, *help me rise*

and water says: *I will.*

Now let us speak of love: Reading Jo Bell's *Kith*

Jo Bell has held numerous poetry residencies, was the inaugural Canal Laureate for the Canal & River Trust, and received an honorary doctorate from the University of Wolverhampton for her services to poetry. Despite this, her two collections *Navigation* (Moormaid Press, 2014), and *Kith* (Nine Arches Press, 2015), attracted scandalously inadequate attention in my view. I'm interested in the latter here, as it's the more substantial volume, with a range of poems that perfectly reflect Bell's interests. Where Selby and Marriott dwell on the enigmas of the non-human, and Calder the mysteries of the human, Bell ponders the emotional connections between the two, always with a strong sense of belonging in nature.

The idea of belonging is suggested by the title, *Kith*, which the *Oxford Language Dictionary* tells us comes from the Old English *cythth*, originally meaning 'knowledge', 'one's native land', and 'friends and neighbours'. For Bell it's about one's connection both to the community and the natural world. This connection is underpinned by love, that elusive abstract noun that features in her opening poem 'Crates'. The poem begins by asking us to imagine crates: 'Observe that when I speak of crates/your mind supplies one straight away', which I really like as an opening: it's a simple statement of fact, in one sense, but it's also a forceful reminder of the power of language. She goes on to list the type of crates that might represent our idea of a crate, then closes with references to the point of the poem: 'Your crate exists as soon as it is thought [...] Now, let us speak of love' [11]. The poem alludes to a cognitive space where such 'existence' is possible, and it's possible because it is a shared experience: we are familiar with both crates and love in at least some of their various forms, but this doesn't mean we think of them, or acknowledge them as often as we might. Bell's final line compels us to 'speak of love', having first reminded us that we *can*: the mind will supply it because we know it, and it can exist for us if we consciously summon it. Love, like an understanding of crates, implies a shared knowledge, and the fact that it's shared enables the connections – the emotional bonding and understanding – that also inform the concept of kith, and make it possible. It's the ideal poem with which to begin the book, because we take this notion with us as we read on, and we feel its relevance again and again throughout.

While love is a permanent possibility, Bell's universe is also one of conflict, which can be seen in many of the book's poems that I don't have space to include here. 'Shame', for instance, depicts a man and woman arguing, and closes with the line, 'We will never know how it is to be kind' [15]. Of course the fact that the speaker has enough understanding of kindness to recognise its absence qualifies the pessimism, but implies that love and kindness are often on shaky ground. Another example is 'Given', a ten-line poem about a relationship with a man on a narrowboat; here are the final five lines:

> We made a travellers' pact to go wherever water let us pass,
> together until each stood in the other's way.
>
> His second gift was a clean parting. Love passes,
> water stays. Inconstant: always borrowed, never spent.
> A better woman would be sorry now. [23]

It should be noted that Jo Bell lives on a narrowboat, and rivers, canals, and water are constant images in her work. In this poem water is the thing that stays as love fades, but water is akin to love in that it's 'never spent'; it's 'Inconstant' only in the sense that it is 'always borrowed'. The final line suggests that she is sanguine about this, and throughout the collection we have the sense that she feels that love and life are about negotiation and compromise: there is always the threat of danger and upset, but the key is to avoid making an obstacle of one's self, and not to stand 'in the other's way'; for Bell, the path of least resistance makes for 'clean parting'. It's the 'natural' path, so to speak, as observed in nature. This can be seen also in a poem called 'I have not asked for this', which closes:

> We know each other best at the beginning
> after all. A little fear will murmur *This will pass:*
> in answer comes a little strength that says
>
> *Then let it pass. But let it pass like Spring* [16]

It's about the breakdown of a relationship, but the identification with nature ameliorates a potentially negative experience: letting it pass 'like Spring' suggests that, while relationships might turn out to be fleeting, transience is as natural as the seasons, and, like the seasons, they also have the potential for renewal. With this more positive mindset we can reinforce our connection to life, and enjoy our relationships with others despite the potential for upset. Another superb poem that explores this idea, and in which her attitude to nature is writ large, is 'Lifted', cited above. It's about canal locks, and takes the form of a conversation between the land and the water. She describes the business of being 'lifted' in a 'mitred lock' by water, which is something that, as a canal dweller, Bell will have experienced numerous times; it's a process of ascent achieved by negotiation, which is expressed brilliantly in the final lines: 'there and here are equal, an imbalance/righted. Ask of it – Water; *help me rise/*and water says: *I will.* [36-37]. When the land makes a polite request of water, water obliges, and this reflects the idea of life as being a negotiation, demanding give and take. It's typical that Bell should create a metaphor linking the natural world with human relationships: it's another example of the spirit of kith that pervades the book and makes it such a well integrated collection. As Jonathan Davidson says, this poem is 'about balance, the give and take, the risk inherent in our daily transfer of emotional energy' that becomes 'a meditation on being human'[21]. Like all of the poems in *Kith* it insists on seeing the human in the broader context of the world beyond ourselves, inviting us to recognise our responsibilities in this relationship.

How Can Poets Use It?

• Bell's work stresses the importance of the self in relation to the world beyond us: while we get the impression that she is brimming with emotion, her reflections on life are outward looking rather than inward looking. Writing about the self, particularly in a confessional way, can sometimes become introspective and self-indulgent, but Bell avoids this by seeking external parallels and real world relevance for the issues that inform her emotional life.

---

[21] Jonathan Davidson, *On Poetry* (Sheffield: Smith/Doorstop Books, 2018), 66-67

Her poetry always has the reader in mind, and is never self-serving.

• Bell is also worth studying for her plain and accessible style, a little like the so-called 'nobrow' poets that I discuss later on. Her points are always made with lucid language, and a narrative approach that often presents poems in the form of fully rendered arguments – as can be seen clearly in 'Crates' and 'Lifted'. In this respect she's very different from a poet like Dixon who, as we've seen, leaves bigger gaps for us to fill; Bell seduces us with fully developed metaphors and conceits that impress us with their fluent and pertinent reasoning.

Writing Prompts

• Read 'Crates' and try to find an object that corresponds to an emotion. Write a poem in which your description/ discussion of that object helps us understand the emotion more fully.

• Read 'Lifted' and try to think of ways in which aspects of the natural world might assist us in our everyday lives. Pick one, and describe an experience that you've had in which you've benefited from nature's 'help'.

Slim Volumes in a Similar Vein

If you enjoyed *Kith* you might also like *Bistro* by Kate North (Cinnamon Press, 2012), *Wanting It* by Diana Whitney (Harbour Mountain Press, 2014), *The Man at the Corner Table* by Rosie

Shepperd (Seren, 2015), *The Book of Tides* by Angela Readman (Nine Arches, 2016), *Terms and Conditions* by Tania Hershman (Nine Arches, 2017), *A Life, Elsewhere* by Marie Naughton (Pindrop Press, 2018), and *Why I Never Finished my Dissertation* by Laura Filey (Headmistress Press, 2019).

PHILOSOPHY I: ETHICS

Where Selby and Marriott explore the non-human, Calder and Bell shift the focus to what it means to be human, raising questions about how we might understand ourselves and our world. Such issues take us into the realm of philosophy, the subject of this section. One of my favourite poetry quotations comes from the American poet Jennifer Grotz who said, 'Poetry is philosophy's sister, the one who wears the make up'[22]. This captures the spirit of poetry as a form that insists on its licence to, as it were, dress-up and flirt, oblivious to pedantic scholars wagging their fingers in judgement. For me poetry embodies rather than rigorously argues its ideas, making them as meaningful as possible by *being* them, unashamedly speaking to the heart along with the head, to the unconscious along with the conscious mind. Here I discuss four poets who explore what we might call 'philosophical' issues without feeling the need to analyse, or indeed to overtly philosophise. Their poems are nevertheless philosophical: dispatches from the front line of ethics, metaphysics, aesthetics, and politics, in that order.

---

[22] From Lance Phillips and Geoffrey Gatza (eds), *Here Comes Everybody: An Anthology* (BlazeVOX, 2005). Later collected in Dennis O'Driscoll (ed), *The Bloodaxe Book of Poetry Quotations* (Bloodaxe, 2006).

PHILOSOPHY I: ETHICS

Victoria Bean's *Liberties*[23]

HE'S BAD

He's bad
he's good
he's misunderstood.

WHO DO YOU LOVE?

Who do you care about, the judge
asks the young person
who nods towards their mum
the judge
says of course, but tell me
who else? Their nan
they say, nans don't judge.

NOTHING HILL

We step back to make way for
the large man cradling
a collection of vinyls to his chest.

We step back again to give
the record shop assistant
the chance to catch him.

---

[23] Victoria Bean, *Liberties* (Ripon: Shoestring Press, 2017). All quotations will be taken from this edition.

SHOES

Now they're with the forensic team
the boy's shoes will tell them
more than he's been willing to.

His young hands too; swabbed with
sterile water and a maternal lightness
as the cotton tip alights on his palm

then strokes the back of his hand
to bring any trace of
the other boy back to life.

Bad, Good, and Misunderstood: Reading Victoria Bean's *Liberties*

Victoria Bean is a visual artist as well as a poet, with a particular interest in concrete poetry – she co-edited *The New Concrete: Visual Poetry in the 21st Century* (2015) with Chris McCabe, and her own visual poetry has been shown at the Tate and the V&A. I'm not concerned with her concrete poetry here, except to note that there is often a strong visual/spatial awareness in her poetry, much of which tends toward minimalism: she likes short poems, surrounded by plenty of white space. There is a strong moral awareness too, and that's what I particularly like about it. Her 2011 collection, *Court*, for instance, draws on the year she spent in Horseferry Road Magistrates' Court, recording the proceedings; the resulting poems often have the feel of verbatim jottings, but there's artistry in the selections, together with a wit and sense of absurdity that makes for a very readable book. The same can be said of the collection I'm interested in here: *Liberties* (2017). Again she's concerned with ethical questions, specifically the sort associated with, to quote the cover blurb, 'trouble – those who cause it, those who are looking for it, and those who have found it'. There are no easy answers, as the six-word poem quoted above, 'He's bad' [50], suggests. The first and second lines of this poem appear to contradict one another, of course, but if we allow that morality is relative, it's perfectly possible to be bad, good, *and* misunderstood simultaneously. The final line feels like the discourse of a social worker, or an apologist for juvenile offenders – essentially it's a cliché, but the poem doesn't give us any context for making judgements about the subject, forcing us to assume that he could be misunderstood by those who think he's bad, *and/or* those who think he's good. The poem's title, 'He's bad' seems like a statement of fact, in which case the final line seeks to excuse someone who may deserve punishment, but it's impossible to say for sure; likewise, the rhyme good/misunderstood offers phonetic closure, but in terms of the moral questions raised there can be none. The only sure thing is that the poem is 'misunderstood' by anyone who assumes he must be one thing or the other. For me it is a neat little statement of moral uncertainty.

Not all of the poems are as short as 'He's bad', but most are fairly succinct, and in a book of over a hundred pages there are plenty of them. If read in isolation some poems may appear trite, but when consumed one after another they have a cumulative effect, gradually eroding any sense of moral certainty we might have. Most feature a similar moral ambivalence, as can be seen in another poem I've included here: 'Who do you love?' This ends with the line 'nans don't judge' [28], which are clearly the sentiments of someone who's never met my nan, but we take the point, and it constitutes another important moral lesson. Usually the better we know someone the more we're likely to understand them on a human level, and the more inclined we are to allow for and forgive their fallibility. Perhaps the implicit question is: should we be judged by detached and objective judges, or by subjective and forgiving nans? To the former we are merely names, but to the latter we are human beings. Can either perspective truly deliver justice? This is the kind of speculation that Bean's terse moral posers trigger for me; the book teems with such tricky ethical questions which are explored with similar pithy detachment.

Another interesting poem I've included above is 'Nothing Hill', describing what appears to be a crime scene, with a 'large man' having stolen some records, chased by a 'shop assistant' [95]. I suppose the moral question here is: which one of these characters would you attempt to step in front of – the thief or the shop assistant pursuing him? Or perhaps like the 'We' of the poem you would let them both past? This poem puts us right at the heart of the action, and makes our moral decision for us. But is it the right one? I expect your answer reflects the kind of person you are; and of course you can't expect a poet to tell you what to do in such situations, certainly not a poet like Bean, who always tends to 'step back' from the issue, remaining scrupulously non-judgemental.

As we see from these examples, Bean's style is plain and ostensibly simple – unlike Marriott she seldom employs elaborate imagery or figurative language – but her skill is in placing appropriate characters in appropriate contexts. Bean's is the poetry of apposite moments, shown but unexplained, inviting her readers to engage in their own way. Consider 'Shoes', about a young offender whose crimes need to be investigated by a 'forensic team' [12]. The implication is that he's killed someone, and now the 'team' need to figuratively 'reconstruct' his victim for the purpose of the investigation.The offender's youth is stressed in the poem, as is the 'maternal' nature of the investigation: the team is like a collection of mothers and midwives, lovingly coaxing the truth from the offender. It's worth noting that the poem has nine lines in total, its form reflecting the nine month duration of a pregnancy: as with many of her poems, the short form complements the subject. But how do we relate to it on a moral and emotional level? Those who coax the truth from the offender are not nurturing parents, they are professionals seeking a conviction, but the maternal references and imagery reminds us that this boy also had a mother, a fact which subtly humanises him in our minds, complicating our emotional response to him, and to those who seek to punish him. It's typical of Bean's deceptively simple poems: they are good at reminding us that human affairs are as complex and mysterious as Marriott's octopus and Calder's brain, often requiring subtle and respectful negotiation, like Bell's canal lock.

How Can Poets Use It?

• As with Marriott, poets who strive for economy should certainly read Bean: she has a real flair for concision, and some of her most powerful poems are haiku-like in their brevity. They rarely feel slight: their force comes from her pithiness and wit, but they also have a narrative dimension. Occasionally they almost resemble microfictions, with a story-like feel underpinned by relatable human conflicts: she is brilliant at identifying and exploiting these, and is able to boil them down to their core, with the essence of each ethical dilemma *becoming* the poem, so-to-speak. However, unlike poets such as Marriott, she rarely relies on figurative language or imagery for effect, demonstrating what can be done with plain diction.

• When I read Bean I'm struck by her ability to keep herself out of her poems: the speaker is generally covert, and she is good at delineating characters and scenarios that speak for themselves, with an inornate, declarative style that perfectly suits her moral purpose.

Writing Prompt

• After rereading all four of Victoria Bean's poems above, imagine you have committed a crime. Write four poems reflecting on the crime: one from the point of view of the victim, one from the victim's mother's perspective, one from your own, and one from the point of view of a judge. Can you fit them together to make a single poem?

• Search the news for a report of a crime, or imagine one for yourself. Try to describe the crime scene as succinctly and objectively as possible in a single stanza.

• Think of a crime and then create a dialogue between a defence lawyer pleading on behalf of the perpetrator, and the prosecution pressing for a conviction.

• After rereading 'Nothing Hill, write a poem that describes a crime, and which involves the reader in the action. Try to work it so that the onus is on the reader to intervene in some way: the second person address 'you' can be useful here.

Slim Volumes in a Similar Vein

If you enjoy Bean's book you might also have a look at *Armadillo Basket* by Helen Buckingham (Waterloo Press, 2011), *Bite Sized* by Fiona Hamilton (Vala Publishing, 2014), *More Than You Were* by Christina Thatcher (Parthian, 2017), *The Cynic in Extremis* by Jacob M. Appel (Able Muse, 2018), *Driver* by Naomi Jaffa (The Garlic Press, 2017), and *Zombies at the Disco* by Alison Stone (Jacar Press, 2020).

PHILOSOPHY II: THE SPIRITUAL

William Orem's *Our Purpose in Speaking*[24]

SONNET: MY MOTHER REFUSES MASTECTOMY

She still believes in Christ, the coloured glass,
leaves coins for saints to find her wandered keys.
When we were boys, I'd watch those gifts amassing
at the marble feet of Anthony,
copper on stone. This season, by some art,
the winter sparrows left their berry shreds
in red striations through her snowy yard.

---

[24] William Orem, *Our Purpose in Speaking* (Wheelbarrow Books: Michigan State University Press, 2018). All quotations will be taken from this edition.

It makes one think of blood – divine, or men's –
one never fully leaves the Catholic dream.
A field of drops on winter snow: a cup:
a cup of bleeding from the whitest fleece.
The hope of worlds beyond this frozen one,

her prayer, at least, for some growth past the suffering.
Outside, all day, the earth dreams of its blossoming.

SONNET: ST FRANCIS TO THE BIRDS

In time, they'll say I came to teach you songs of mine:
a canticle of suffering, and tears
around a thorny head in Palestine.
You birds, it is not so. I come to hear.
Grant me whatever grace is there inside your breasts
and drives the happy life from which you grow.
Grant me the blue heart tapping in the sheltered nest,
the subtle flutes and filters of your bones.
With broken sighs my brothers march their broken way;
with lamentation, take to dirty knees.
But I myself shall bow this day
among the tents of feathered ministry,

for I have found you crying hopeful airs
superior to prayer. You birds, I come to hear.

SNOWFALL EXPECTED AFTER MIDNIGHT

Stepping outside I am struck quite still and dumb by cold
the way nocturnal creatures nestled in the crooks of barns

and hollow boles across the mile-long, empty field must,
I think, be wakened sometimes

by nothing at all,
only the endless, consecutive Sabbath of night –

its deep blue excellence – and the voice,
no voice really, of something just past animal sense:

more a kind of yearning, perhaps, or that flexed sensation
in the hindpart of the ear

when we expect a word, but no word comes, and so instead
we hear our own listening. How they must go tense

on such nights, field mice furrowed under grass,
chipmunks hid in frosty strips of earth and weed;

or, like the owls with their great soft heads,
all pupil, each retinal cell awakened now to magnify

the heavens' ever-novel blank-exquisite dark-
merely held in cold

suspension;
until they vault into it, each to instinct's end,

the moment passed. Or, possibly,
the moment clutched, its tiny heart mad against the claw;

for this night is knowing nothing
that we do not actually know: simple hunger, simple lust,

nature's ground rules, kill and swallow, cough the bones,
be still, and watch.

Worlds Beyond This Frozen One: Reading William Orem's *Our Purpose in Speaking*

For Victoria Bean philosophical issues are all grounded in secular reality, but I'll now look at a book which moves beyond the mundane world, exploring the relevance of the metaphysical: William Orem's first collection, *Our Purpose in Speaking*.

Particularly striking for me is how the spiritual is addressed from a very personal perspective. The sample sonnet, 'My Mother Refuses Mastectomy', for instance, explores his mother's Catholic faith, and how this defines her life, and death. It's about the weight of the past on the present, specifically the significance of the 'Catholic dream' as a life-shaping narrative. As a traditional form the sonnet is perhaps appropriate for a poem *about* tradition. The regular pulse of the iambic line and the conventions it invokes reflects the notion of convention in our lives: like the iambic beat that is so close to ordinary speech, traditions perist beneath the surface of our lives, often barely noticed. Certainly tradition shapes the mother's thinking here, reinforcing her adherence to the rituals of her faith, which some may see as superstitions. St Anthony is the patron saint of lost things, but the mother hasn't lost her faith, and she maintains her belief in his influence. Her son's perspective is more sceptical, perhaps, but even he is moved to interpret the juice of the berries in biblical terms, as suggested by the imagined transubstantiation of juice into blood, underpinning his mother's 'hope of worlds beyond this frozen one' [3], and perhaps his own hope too. The final line of the poem links the possibility of an afterlife with the earth's 'dreams' of forthcoming rebirth: they are dreams which, as we know, come true in a sense every spring, so perhaps mother and son's spiritual dreams will also blossom?

The closing couplet of the sonnet implies a degree of optimism, then, but elsewhere in the book spiritual and filial concerns are explored with more scepticism, and occasionally darkness. His free verse poem 'Critical Care' is unfortunately too long to include here in full, but it's one which unpacks the speaker's relationship with his mother in a more detailed and nuanced way. Here the dying mother has a history of alcohol abuse, and we learn that she ill-treated her son in his youth, who uses words like '*wicked* and *rotten* and *shame*' in his account of their relationship [35]. Thus the notion of 'critical care' extends beyond healthcare to parental responsibility, with the mother seen as wanting in her role; criticism also extends to religion, represented by a hospital priest who is indicted for being 'far too chipper', and who hovers at the mother's bedside, 'full of inaccessible smiles' [37]. We're in no doubt by the time we finish the poem that care, both parental and spiritual, are 'critical', but people often struggle to provide it. His mother 'drank herself into the rug', while the priest, who should offer comfort on her deathbed, cannot make an appropriate connection, remaining as remote and inaccessible as the God he represents. But there is also ambivalence to be found in the poem: while the speaker refers to his mother as 'my hated mother', he nevertheless begs her not to die, and seeks a form of 'consolation' through language, as here in the closing stanzas:

> This is my mother;
> these are my best reassurances to her;
> this is the way we speak

as if we had found consolation,
as if the narrow cracker between tongue
and palette were, in fact, a door. [37]

The book's title is *Our Purpose in Speaking*, and we get a sense of a possible purpose here – to achieve the 'consolation' that might be found in speech: the word that might open 'a door' to a reconciliation that matches the speaker's needs. However, the reiterated phrase 'as if' suggests that this is more hope than reality. The poet's need to voice his love for his mother, and to believe in her worth, is set against his struggles to relinquish past resentments – this ambivalence creates a forceful tension that becomes a feature of this poem, and many others in the book.

Though ambivalence and scepticism persistently qualify the sentiments expressed in *Our Purpose*, there's always a willingness to entertain hope, and to acknowledge the relevance and potency of the spiritual life, both in terms of religious myth, and the presence of the ineffable. This can be seen to wonderful effect in sonnets like 'Francis to the Birds', where bird song takes the place of prayer in the mind of St Francis: the poem's closing lines address the birds directly, 'for I have found you crying hopeful airs/superior to prayer' [41]. Here the natural world is viewed through the lens of religion, privileging the former: the oxymoron 'crying hopeful' is typical of Orem, suggesting unrequited spiritual need – it's a world where truth and meaning are inaccessible via religious institutions, but he feels they may exist regardless.

The other poem I've chosen to include in full, 'Snowfall Expected After Midnight', clearly invokes the natural world for a spiritual purpose, referencing the 'nocturnal creatures nestled in the crooks of barns' which seem to communicate without a voice: rather than conventional speech there's 'something just past animal sense:/ more a kind of yearning' about their messages [4-5]. The poem implies that these creatures are like us, animated by forces beyond their understanding, and beyond expression – they have 'no voice', and nothing namable to articulate, but the mysterious 'yearning' or 'sensation' that informs their lives is real, and the wildlife respond to it. The poem goes on to suggest that humans would 'expect a word' for this, but 'no word comes'; yet meaning seems to endure beyond language, manifest in the lifeforce itself, and in this sense at least the mystery *isn't* a mystery ('nothing/that we do not actually know'). The poem implies that we must learn to trust 'nature's ground rules', learn through observing and partaking in the world of which we are a part – this sounds vague, of course, and Orem is only ever gesturing toward meaning. As readers we are in the position of Orem's wildlife: invited to *feel* the meanings that we don't quite have the language for.

Orem strikes me as a spiritual person who is disenchanted with religion and religious institutions; we feel his desire for a spiritual language that transcends them: in other words to find a 'purpose in speaking'. Reading Orem I am occasionally reminded of the British poet Michael Symmons Roberts, who one critic described as an author of 'secular prayers': this might be a good term for Orem's tentative gestures toward the spiritual.[25] I'm also reminded of something the American poet Charles Simic once said, 'The task of poetry, perhaps, is to salvage a trace of the authentic from

[25] Reviewing Michael Symmons Roberts' book, *Drysalter*, Kate Kellaway called his poems 'secular prayers', and 'disciplined exaltation', https://www.theguardian.com/books/2013/apr/22/drysalter-michael-symmons-roberts-review

the wreckage of religious, philosophical, and political systems'[26]. This also appears to be part of Orem's unspoken agenda in this strange and beautiful slim volume.

How Can Poets Use It?

• Orem works well within traditional forms, and his sonnets in particular are worthy of close scrutiny for poets, particularly for the way he manages to marry form and theme, as seen in 'My Mother Refuses Mastectomy' and 'St Francis to the Birds'.

• Unlike Victoria Bean, we feel the poet's subjective presence strongly in Orem's writing – we sense his emotional engagement with his poems, but while he deals with traumatic events that sometimes involve bitterness and recrimination, his treatment feels measured. This is because he is careful to admit his own subjectivity and uncertainty, particularly involving his ambivalence toward his mother and her beliefs. He signals his emotional fragility, and the complexity of the filial and spiritual issues he raises: there's a sense in which he humanises his subjects by showing himself as human.

• Orem will be of particular interest to poets looking for ways to address spiritual concerns: in one sense this is a theme for which a language doesn't exist, and this, as suggested, is Orem's principal concern in his book. I'd recommend him to those who sense spiritual truths beneath

[26] Charles Simic, *A Fly In the Soup* (University of Michigan Press, 2002), 160

the veneer of mundane reality, and who feel the need to write about them: Orem can help, perhaps, not because he solves the problem of capturing the ineffable in art, but because he turns the problem itself into art.

Writing Prompts

• Write a poem asking St Anthony to find something important that you've lost. You don't have to be a Catholic to do this, of course (poetry lends itself to scepticism as much as to faith). Try using different 'lost' items until you find one that feels significant to you, then pursue that significance as far as you can.

• After reading 'St Francis to the Birds' and 'Snowfall Expected After Midnight', imagine that an animal is trying to communicate with you in order to tell you something meaningful about life. What form might its language take, and what might it tell you?

Slim Volumes in a Similar Vein

If you enjoy Orem's book you might also like *In A Hare's Eye* by Breda Wall Ryan (Doire Press, 2015), *Dear Big Gods* by Mona Arshi (Liverpool University Press, 2019), *Leaves* by Matthew Hollis (Hazel Press, 2020) , *A Sense of Tiptoe* by Karen Hayes (Holland Park Press, 2020) *Sehnsucht* by Christine McNeill (Shoestring Press, 2020), and *Religious Poems, Maybe* by John Powell Ward (Cinnamon Press, 2020).

PHILOSOPHY III: AESTHETICS

Nadine Brummer's *Whatever It Is that Chimes*[27]

AT THE LUCIAN FREUD EXHIBITION

Head, hands, genitals and feet
are main events – he does them well.
Excess between is fleshed like meat.

And even now it takes some nerve to look
at turkey gizzard limp between men's legs
and woman opening to a swarm of black.

Oh there's a buzz all right. Once at another show
I heard a woman in a hat enthuse
about a clever orchid, how

lips form a helipad for flies
which land in ruts, and trapped then sucked
where male and female parts are fused,

though none are needed for the helleborine
quite self-sufficient with its seed.
Can flowers be both gorgeous and obscene?

Leigh Bowery's back is overgrown with flecks,
an orchidaceous pink, buttocks sag
into an off-white stool. You sense the cracks

---

[27] Nadine Brummer, *Whatever It Is that Chimes: New and Selected Poems* (Nottingham: Shoestring Press, 2020). All quotations will be taken from this edition.

of old enamel bowls and chipped chrome taps
behind a drape. In front a red-brown rug
bristles. These genteel props

touch my eyes. Below each covering a frame,
upholding surfaces of this and that,
lies coiled, and I am forced to look again

at how I live. This cold October day
I'm in a crowd well heeled and buttoned up
engrossed with such carnality

I fear our coats might flake and tear
and eyes, preoccupied with doubt,
find bodies we'd not bargained for.

THE FROG'S PRINCESS

That night, finding him in my bed,
within kissing distance,
I wanted to take the stare
off his face – those eyes
all bulge and goggle.
Then I saw their depth, a look
that could take me anywhere
backwards in time. I recalled
an aquarium under the sea where
I'd pressed my face to the glass
of a wolf-eel's tank, mesmerised
by a little reptilian head
with eyeballs lifting off
like spaceships that settled
into an expression beyond
a seal-pup's dopey smile
or the pout of fish –

like that of some new-born child
you swear has been here before.
The frog was like him,
but when he gulped and a mouth
smelling of weed or bull-kelp
came close to my lips
I flinched and held out my hand
to stop his jump and touched
a spasm of green, a creature trying
to slither out of himself.
I've been so often trapped
In flesh that didn't feel mine
I wondered what he could see
when he gazed into a pond;
he took my sigh as a signal
to kiss. I loved him best
the moment before he changed,
a small, crouched, alien thing
in need of a body.

Bodies We'd Not Bargained For: Reading Nadine Brummer's *Whatever It Is that Chimes*

Manchester born Nadine Brummer's first chapbook, *A Question of Blue Tulips*, appeared in 1998, and a first full collection, *Half Way to Madrid*, in 2002. The latter was a Poetry Book Society Recommendation, and subsequent collections have also been well-received, yet in my view she still doesn't have the profile she deserves as poet. *Whatever It Is that Chimes: New and Selected Poems* (2020), is the best introduction to her work.

You'll notice from the poems above that Brummer enjoys close observation and sustained philosophical reflection. I place her in the category of 'aesthetics' because she often focuses on art and culture; she is a wonderful ekphrastic poet, adept at feeding off the creative work of others and using it to deepen her understanding of the world. 'At the Lucian Freud Exhibition' is a good example of a poem that uses painting as inspiration, moving beyond a simple description of the artwork to the exhibition itself as an event. We know what Lucian Freud's paintings look like, of course, but Brummer is interested in what it means to like them. We're told that it takes 'nerve to look/at turkey gizzard limp between men's legs/and women opening to a swarm of black' [3], but our eyes are drawn despite ourselves. The bodies we have 'not bargained for', in all their grotesque reality, are our own, and Brummer implies that we are driven by a fascination with the things that we force into the unconscious; we 'fear' them, but we are nevertheless engrossed. This fear suggests more than mere physical squeamishness; it's a fundamental conflict at the heart of our psyche. Brummer's fellow art lovers are straight-laced ('buttoned up') and privileged ('well heeled'), and the high brow art exhibition is an expression of their civilised and sophisticated lives, but a sense of their own carnality threatens their world: it implies an unsettling truth lies beneath the veneer. This truth is central to the speaker's 'doubt', and the tension we feel when we read the poem.

Brummer uses art to learn about herself and her world, and her insights are sometimes psychological, sometimes political, sometimes spiritual. The latter is explored in several poems not cited here, including 'First Books' where she describes reading an illustrated edition of the bible as a young girl. It was a present from her aunt, 'inscribed' and 'gold-tooled', and we're told that it's one of the earliest art artefacts to capture her imagination, 'the biggest book I owned/as a child'. Given Brummer's Jewish heritage, she felt guilty when reading the books of the New Testament, which she'd peruse furtively like pornography; as with Lucien Freud's artwork, the speaker of this poem perceives something taboo in art, and struggles to assess its meaning in the final stanza of the poem:

> How had I learned to dread Jesus?
> No-one I remember had said
> I must run past Brideoak Street's convent
> as if someone was out to get me.
> To this day I brood on Jesus –
>
> who on earth did he think he was? [119]

Brummer's poems often end like this, with the poet pondering what art and culture can tell her about herself and the human condition, and this frequently involves the kind of ambivalence we see here. The ostensibly scornful final line implicitly acknowledges the significance of the very thing it appears to criticise, given that she continues to 'brood' in the present (she wouldn't brood if she didn't care). The line raises several questions at once: is she asking 'who on earth' did Jesus think he was in making himself so appealing in her copy of the New Testament? Or 'who on earth' did he think he was claiming to be the Son of God? This is clever writing, and the phrase 'on earth' (reflecting the language of the Lord's Prayer) is skillfully employed to generate an irony that reflects the complexity of the questions she raises: we don't know the answer to either, but we *do* feel that the 'brooding'

Brummer thought he was something noteworthy, and still does. Ultimately she seems to be asking a question about herself: whether the force of her response to the New Testament is due to her status as Jewish which, like Orem's Catholicism, continues to assert its influence in maturity.

Brummer is inspired by other art forms too, including myths and folktales. A poem that illustrates Brummer's interest in inherited stories, for instance, is 'The Frog's Princess', which I've included above. It draws on the fairy tale collected by the Brothers Grimm, 'The Frog Prince', and it demonstrates Brummer's talent for textured language and evocative imagery: note, for instance, the description of the frog's face, 'all bulge and goggle'. The reference to the aquarium that follows this line takes us on a journey into the speaker's own unconscious, which in turn implies a *collective* unconscious: the 'reptilian head' which is both alien and familiar ('like that of some new-born child/you swear has been here before'), suggesting the kind of pervasive symbolism we often sense in fairy tales. She includes the reader in this with her use of the second person, 'you', underlining the idea of a ubiquitous identification, a shared significance. Notice too how Brummer identifies most with the frog the 'moment before' he changed into a prince; she identifies with its vulnerability and need, and perhaps also with the anticipation of change itself, rather than the reality of life after the fairy tale ends. The body of a handsome prince does not necessarily imbue an individual with value in Brummer's world; he had more worth as a creature that she could learn from, symbolic of her own alienation, perhaps: her own desire for metamorphosis into a more comfortable body, and her need to jettison 'flesh that didn't feel mine'.

Thus Brummer uses existing art for philosophical and creative purposes, and her interpretive lens is fundamental to her aesthetic. From Lucien Freud to the Brothers Grimm, she employs the art of the past to assist her interrogation of the present.

How Can Poets Use It?

• Brummer shows us ways in which we can use our consumption of art to fuel our own creative lives. We all do this to a degree – it's impossible for writers to detach themselves from history and their own cultural consumption – but Brummer often makes it explicit, creating dialogues with existing art that lead in new and exciting directions. Brummer often views her own life through the lens of art, offering an interpretative account of what she sees, but also reflecting on the psychological implications; she frequently strives to understand herself through art, and I think poets can learn a lot from how she approaches this.

• Brummer is adept at using irony to create ambiguity, as seen at the end of 'First Books' discussed above, and she's also good at using doubt as a creative spur: her uncertainty about subjects like sex, religion, and art often seems to provide the catalyst for her writing; she demonstrates how it's possible to use the tensions and conflicts they create in ways that feel both edifying and cathartic .

Writing Prompts

• Next time you're at a public gathering such as an art exhibition, a concert, or a football match, observe the other people present and write a poem about why you think they're there. As with 'At the Lucian Freud Exhibition', try to push your questioning beyond the obvious answers (i.e. because they like art, music, or football), and consider how the pastime might relate to their identity, or their sense of meaning in the world.

• After reading 'The Frog's Princess', take your favourite (or least favourite) fairy tale and rewrite it as a poem, changing the gender of either the hero or the villain of the story.

• Imagine waking up in a fairy tale of your choice, then write a poem about the characters you encounter. Write from the perspective of the real world (ie the world you live in rather than the fairy tale universe).

Slim Volumes in a Similar Vein

If you enjoy Brummer's collection, particularly the art-based facet of her work, you might also like *Cur* by Martin Malone (Shoestring, 2015), *Pike in the Carp Pond* by Pnina Shinebourne (Smokestack, 2017), *Chagall's Circus* by William Bedford (Dempsey & Windle, 2019) and *After Hopper and Lange* by David Olsen (Oversteps Books, 2021).

PHILOSOPHY IV: POLITICS

Politics has a bearing on everything, of course, and modern poetry addresses diverse political issues in a host of ways. When people speak about 'political' poetry they often mean poetry addressing social justice issues like race, gender, sexuality, and the environment; however, for many poets, politics is chiefly about class, economics and the alienating potential of work: certainly this is the case in Graham Fulton's funny slim volume, *Open Plan.*

Graham Fulton's *Open Plan*[28]

DARK MATTER

the lights are asleep
　and
the switched off office
　　is tingling
　with all
the passwords
　waiting to be changed
and the toilets
　　waiting to be flushed
and the numbers
　　　waiting to be crunched
and the clocks
　　　waiting to be watched
and the systems
　　　waiting to be crashed
and the bucks
　　waiting to be passed

---

[28] Graham Fulton, *Open Plan* (Ripon: Smokestack Books, 2011). All quotations will be taken from this edition.

and
a space
        waiting to be filled
and the holes
            waiting
to be black.

FOOD CHAIN

the Serengeti
  open plan office
is sliced into
    hard little pods
which are diced
        into hard little
work stations
            with all new desks
and all old chairs
        on which we perch
in a theoretically
        ergonomically friendly way
with our backs exposed
        which goes against our need
for defensible space
        in case a lion or wolf decides
to hunt us for lunch with only
    our paper clips and protractors and
correction fluid for weapons.

ALIEN NATION

Tony Loony
        takes a
well–earned break

from
    creating
committee deadline reports
  and lifts the lid
of the scanner
     slaps his face
down on the glass
and happily
commences
     to scan
it
   while
shoogling
   his head about
to make him look
   like a Martian
from *The Outer Limits.*

The New Proletariat: Reading Graham Fulton's *Open Plan*

Graham Fulton is a Scot who's been writing poetry since the late
80s, issuing numerous books with a wide range of publishers.
Among other things, he is known for his ability to exploit the
rhythms of the Scottish vernacular, together with a sharp and often
mordant wit. He frequently writes about place, and has a talent for
identifying the characters that help define a region, particularly
his home town of Paisley, which he explores vividly and hilariously
in collections like *Chips, Paracetamol and Wine* (Smokestack,
2020). However, the book I'm interested in here, *Open Plan*
(Smokestack, 2011), takes the modern office as its subject. Its
contention is that 'White-collar workers are the new proletariat',
and cumulatively his poems construct a story of a working office

with the satirical feel of Ricky Gervais's mockumentary, *The Office*.

Open Plan reveals that the 'new proletariat' is as alienated as the old proletariat. The opening poem, 'dark matter', sets the scene expertly: notice how the office is anthropomorphised, but human only insofar as it feels its own misery; its early morning 'tingling' anticipates the irritations of the modern working day, a far cry from the ennobling dignity of fulfilling employment. The empty office demands 'to be filled', awaiting the day as the universe might await its own annihilation: the phrase 'waiting/to be black' [11] sounds like a longing for oblivion. You'll also notice Fulton's distinctive style, with its apparently simple descriptions of everyday situations. He takes his lead from poets such as the American blue-collar author Charles Bukowski – like Bukowski he is adept at finding humour in alienation. You can sense connections with other American poets too, like the Detroit-born poet of the working classes, Philip Levine, and, particularly, Fred Voss, whose verse charts working life at the imaginary Goodstone Aircraft Company. Gerald Locklin once praised Voss for possessing 'the subtle ear of a true free-versifier'[29], and Fulton has this too – the seemingly formless, informal style which often has the patina of conversational speech.

The poem 'food chain' above suggests that the open plan office is designed in an ostensibly 'ergonomically friendly way', but with their 'backs exposed' the staff's sense of security is violated, along with their instinctive 'need/for defensive space' [13]. The office becomes a figurative Serengeti, with employees at the mercy of the 'lions and the wolves' who might 'hunt us for lunch'. He develops

---

[29] See Locklin's preface to the 1991 Bloodaxe edition of Fred Voss's *Goodstone*.

this idea in several poems that I haven't room to cite in full here, such as 'bad magnet' where we learn that the pernicious hunters include colleagues who engage in inane conversation or humourless humour, arriving at workstations to 'sing/the *Stingray* theme tune/ or make twittering noises/or talk about/how useless/everyone else in the world is ['bad magnet', 65]. In the poem 'new start' we learn that it's a place where 'people begin their jobs/with great expectations' but soon develop 'workhorse expressions/that clearly say/*Dear God/please let me die* ['new start', 64].

The open plan office isn't conducive to the formation of relationships, then, or indeed to any kind of efficiency: colleagues and work are mere irritations to characters like 'Mick the Stick' who, in the poem 'resigner bubble', 'doesn't care/that those he's meant/to supervise/spend half their time/chatting on the phone/ [...]/because/he's got a new job/and very soon he'll never see/any of them/ever/again' ['resigner bubble', 61]. Mick is one of numerous office types that we might recognise from popular culture, but Fulton's workers are distinctive enough to avoid cliché.

They include characters like 'Bob the bigboned receptionist' ['people skills'], 'Katie the existential typist' ['special k'], and 'Alan Seedy McCready' ['down size']. The latter has 'a rare genetic condition/which has left him/smaller than normal' and so he has 'decided/to christen himself a himp/which is a cross between/a hobbit and a chimp' [16]. While the employees dream of a life elsewhere, readers are left wondering about the alternatives that the modern world might offer. This is the point of poems like 'royal court' where the character 'Prince John' 'announces/that he's going/home early to watch *Big Brother*/because *there's so much more/to life than THIS*' [21] – this is typical of Fulton's withering irony, and his point is that sometimes we are slaves to our own lack of imagination, which makes the possibility of escape even more difficult.

Many Fulton characters desperately seek to transform themselves and each other, either literally or metaphorically: in 'paper jam' [52] employees see their 'ridiculous contorted faces/snarling back at' them from the photocopier; in 'block buster' 'King Man' sees all his colleagues as *Star Wars* characters; in 'alien nation', quoted in full above, 'Tony Loony' transforms himself into an alien because he is alienated from his own life: like Karl Marx's alienated workers, the open plan employees have lost agency – they are economic entities whose destiny is shaped by faceless forces beyond their control; they are alienated from the processes that govern their lives, and from their own humanity. In this respect it's notable that the function of the office is never stated – we don't know the purpose of the number-crunching, or the photocopying, or the phrenetic keyboard activities, and we have the impression that the staff don't either; certainly they don't seem to care: the only thing that motivates them is a desire to escape. In 'alien nation' Tony Loony signals his alienation by making himself resemble a Martian, one assumes because he has reached 'the outer limit' of his sanity.

Once more the poems in this slim volume are best read alongside one another: they combine to create a kind of fragmentary novella, offering a strong sense of place and a darkly humorous story of modern working life – it's a story that leads nowhere, but then that's its point.

How Can Poets Use It?

• In *Open Plan* Fulton's aesthetic is driven mainly by humour, as opposed to, say, cadence or imagery. Rather like Franz Kafka, he has the knack of making alienation funny: poets will find it useful to study his use of comic metaphors, and his skilful way of employing hyperbole and incongruity for comic effect (it's incongruous, for instance, for adults to sing the *Stingray* theme tune in the workplace!) He uses well chosen comic details to augment the sense of absurdity in his writing, without undermining the authentic feel of the world he describes.

• Writers like Fulton remind us of the poetic potential that exists in the mundane world. In some ways, it's hard to think of an environment less inspiring than an open plan office, but Fulton transforms it into a fit subject for art. The implicit political underpinning provides significance for his poems, and adds depth to the theme of entrapment, while the humour makes them eminently readable and entertaining.

• Poets would do well to pay close attention to Fulton's lineation – notice, for instance, the dropped lines in the poems cited above. This slows down the reading process, deepening our engagement with the scenes he constructs, and increasing our sense that we are reading art rather than mere anecdotes.

Writing Prompts

• Think of some of the characters who occupy your own workplace, and write a poem which exaggerates their defining traits for comic effect. Try setting characters who love their jobs alongside those who don't.

• Fulton often uses metaphor to describe the experience of the modern workplace (see his references to the Serengeti, *Star Wars*, etc). With this in mind, write a poem that creates an effective comparison for your own job.

Slim Volumes in a Similar Vein

If you enjoy *Open Plan* you might also like *Harmonica* by Geoff Hattersley (Wrecking Ball Press, 2003), *Being Present* by Neil Elder (Black Light Engine Room Press, 2017), *Roar* by Martin Hayes (Smokestack, 2018), *In Retail* by Jeremy Dixon (Arachne Press, 2019), and *Shop TALK* by Paul Tanner (Penniless Press, 2019).

REGIONS I: THE POLITICS AND POETICS OF PLACE

Places signify in numerous ways for poets: as we've seen, the open plan office is clearly a significant place for writers like Fulton, defining the working lives of modern white-collar workers and creating a community of the oppressed. Now I'll turn to poetry's relationship with geographical regions, beginning with two collections that were inspired partly by the conflicts associated with historically disputed territory.

Annemarie Ní Churreáin's *Bloodroot*[30]

BORDER

At first I knew nothing of the border
or that I was being divided

from my own kind, women
who like me possess the earth

in their eyes,
the steep incline of mountains, valleys, wells.

Now, I trace the curves of shoulders,
in foundling photographs,

hems of hair that sweep towards the sun.
And I recall the plovers

on the heather-hill behind our house
each year, a cloak

of peat-gold wings flocking the sky
like mirrors.

BOG MEDICINE

Drink these star-leafed nettles
and keep in your purse a fern.

To become invisible, say your harm
to the hill.

---

[30] Annemarie Ní Churreáin, *Bloodroot* (Connemara: Doire Press, 2017). All quotations will be taken from this edition.

This hill is pagan
This hill is Hill.

It will answer in bog-tongue
and occasional fire,
burning back the earth
along the heather-stream

despite bald heels of rock,
despite the kissy mink,
despite a saintly air

until the stream runs dark
with what needs
to blacken out of you.

Restore Us Back Into the Landscape: Reading Annemarie Ní Churreáin's *Bloodroot*

In this debut collection Annemarie Ní Churreáin finds meaning
in her ambivalent relationship with place, specifically the region
of her birth in North West Donegal. This is a coastal region
characterised by rural landscapes, small villages, and, not least, its
proximity to the contested region of Northern Ireland. An
awareness of the border between North and South is at the heart
of much tension in her work, as can be seen in 'Border', with the
poet's realisation that she 'was being divided' by place and the
conflicts she's inherited [26]. The divided Ireland is perceived as
an imposition that violates the speaker's connection to the land,
and her sense of belonging and ownership. Such connections are
vital to Ní Churreáin, inextricably related to her identity and values.

Notice how she reinforces this idea by stressing the connection between the land and the people – we're told that the women possess the earth 'in their eyes', and their 'hems of hair' which 'sweep towards the sun': she presents the division of the land almost as a physical assault on the body, rather than just an affront to identity, or a mere geographical demarcation.

The English poet Roy Fisher once said of his home city, Birmingham, that: 'Birmingham is what I think with'[31], and the same could be said of Ní Churreáin's relationship with place, as implied in many poems that I don't have space to include in full here, including 'House', in which she writes,

> On that grave, bare soil I could return completely,
> feel my way back towards the centre as a blind woman might,
> with only love as her guide. [27]

The reference to 'love' clearly underscores her emotional bond to place, but ambivalence is rarely far away. The negative aspects of place aren't always the fault of a physical border, but sometimes result from the parochialism of the small town experience, as seen in a poem like 'Scandal', from which I include two stanzas:

> The villagers did not unite
> in outrage
> but instead, they set about their days as usual,
> posting letters, buying fruit, forming queues in the bank after lunchtime.

---

[31] See, '"Birmingham's what I think with": Roy Fisher's Composite-Epic', *The Yale Journal of Criticism*, 13, 2000, 105 - 87

They said *little*
but within that *little* lay much:
little was a gated field in which something extraordinary was buried.
[39]

The implication is that a local 'scandal' is augmented by an inability to voice it, particularly in the 'gated field' of such a conventional, insular life. The cause is often bigotry born of patriarchy, and for Ní Churreáin Irish history is characterised by an inability to cope with female transgression, particularly in the form of extramarital sex and illegitimate childbirth; consider the predicament addressed in this extract from 'Penance':

'Shame'.
    Use this word when you speak of love.

A man of cloth will come.
Your new home is among brides.

Deny
the child inside you is the child you dream at night [23]

This legacy of shaming and exclusion contributes to the poet's ambivalence, then, becoming a creative spur for much of her writing. She makes meaning from the conflicts that are related to place, and her love for her region is countered by her need to voice a long overdue sense of outrage.

Ní Churreáin is interested in how the landscape of her native Ireland shapes the community, and her, but she is also concerned with what is buried beneath it, both figuratively and literally. This can be seen in the poem 'The Kerry Foot', which references the

'Kerry Babies' case that saw a woman accused of killing her newborn baby in the 1980s. Speaking of this poem in one interview, Ní Churreáin says,

> It was written at Cahir Saidhbhín, a place that translates from Irish as 'Fort of Little Sadbh'. In legend Sadbh was robbed by a spurned suitor of her human body and separated from her young child. It was this legend that helped me explore another story local to that same site, that of the 1984 'Kerry Babies'.[32]

Thus her poem links a modern atrocity with enduring myths of place; her objective, as she says elsewhere, is to 'unbury us and restore us back into the landscape to which we truly belong, placing the body back at the centre of human experience, placing human experience back at the centre of the State'[33] This 'unburying' requires both psychological and political adjustments: we must confront uncomfortable (buried) truths, and work to establish a state of understanding. In some poems, restoring 'us back into the landscape to which we truly belong' means recognising the connections between the human and the nonhuman, as in 'Bog Medicine' which I've included in full above. Here she breaks down the distinction between the self and the natural world. The poem seems to suggest that, if we seek our answers in the landscape ('say your harm/to the hill' [20]), it replies, absorbing our 'harm' in its cleansing and restorative waters. She appears to have in mind a

---

[32] See 'Poets on Poetry' interview in *Island's Edge*, https://www.islandsedgepoetry.net/poets-a-j/annemarie-n%C3%AD-churre%C3%A1in/

[33] Annemarie Ní Churreáin, 'I was raised in the shadow of men who wanted to conquer wildness', *The Irish Times*, Oct 26, 2017. https://www.irishtimes.com/culture/books/i-was-raised-in-the-shadow-of-men-who-wanted-to-conquer-wildness-1.3268313

form of Celtic ethnomedicine – an animistic healing process underpinned by the belief in a ubiquitous and accessible spiritual energy. I like this idea. To benefit from 'bog medicine' we must meet the landscape halfway – drink its 'star-leaved nettles' and cherish its precious ferns; we must cultivate our relationship with the natural world, and learn to adjust our ears to 'bog-tongue'; of course this is figurative language, suggesting a shift in mindset: in short she urges us to adjust to wildness, rather than attempt to 'conquer' it, sentiments that align her with the eco-poets addressed earlier in this book.

How Can Poets Use It?

• Ní Churreáin makes the connections between the self and her region meaningful, personalising and dramatising an inherited political conflict. We have the impression that she feels it at a visceral level. Everyone's association with place[s] is political in a sense, and this book reveals compelling ways of interrogating that experience, unpacking the implications, and turning them into art.

• Ní Churreáin is another poet who is very conscious of the sound of words, and she uses repetition and alliteration to superb effect. Notice the repetitions in 'Bog Medicine', for instance, which makes use of the so-called 'rule of three', with the reiteration of 'hill' in stanza three and 'despite' in stanza five: the count of three feels right in this context, and demonstrates the poet's ear for timing. She also has an excellent ear and eye for adjectives – poets need to be sparing with adjectives because they have a tendency to draw attention to themselves, but again Ní Churreáin chooses carefully, with her references to, for example, 'bald heels of rock', 'kissy mink', etc, she creates texture without excess.

Writing Prompts

• Research the history of the region in which you live, focusing particularly on its myths and legends. Think of the ways in which they might relate to your sense of place in the modern world. Write a poem that attempts to bring one of those old stories to bear on the present.

• Think of the most notable violent act to have taken place in your region. Reflect on how this might be made meaningful: is it symbolic of a broader violence (think perhaps in terms of ideology: imperialism, racism, patriarchy, etc)?

• Reread 'Bog Medicine' and imagine there is a cure for something that ails you to be found in the place of your birth. What could that be? Write a poem that describes your attempts to find it.

Slim Volumes in a Similar Vein

If you enjoy the themes of *Bloodroot*, particularly its focus on place, you might also like *Majuba Road* by Julie Hogg (Vane Women Press, 2016), *Dogtooth* by Fran Lock (Out-Spoken Press, 2017), *The Hill* by Angela France (Nine Arches Press, 2017), *The Work of a Winter* by Maureen Boyle (Arlen House, 2018), and

Listening to the Night by Jane Routh (Smith/Doorstop, 2018).
Those interested in the relationship between place and gender might
enjoy *London Undercurrents: The Hidden Histories of London's
Unsung Heroines, North and South of the River*, a collaborative
project by Joolz Sparkes and Hilaire (Holland Park Press, 2019),
and *Carnivorous* by Moyra Donaldson (Doire Press, 2019).

Gary Allen's *Jackson's Corner*[34]

THE TEMPLE BUILDERS

My father and I were never close
it seemed, after the first child, he simply gave up
parenthood wasn't he'd signed up for
the grinning football matches
the military Life Boy parades
the glen caravan holidays he never went on.

He used to look in silent vexation
at the boys wrestling on the mat
the only girl becoming something obscene
as he sighed and made the manly pilgrimage
from work, to pub, from betting-shop, to bed.

I knew only an angry frustrated voice
as solemn as the biblical words in the King James
as my grandfather's God-fearing announcements
just before he died covered in clotted blood.

Hold the bloody light still, in the name of God, he cursed
the screwdriver blade slipping

---

[34] Gary Allen, *Jackson's Corner* (London: Greenwich Exchange, 2016), 34. All further
quotations will be taken from this edition.

out of a screw groove too wide
and the strange oozing of blood from a white hand
repulsively intimate, the food reeking-breath
the touch of his flesh as he reached over me.

Holy Jesus, you useless bloody shite, as I let the bracket
slip beneath my childish grasp
as he flung the bracket and connections to the floor
lit a Woodbine between trembling lips –

both failures, he stunned me into awed confusion
by slipping a still-hot silver sixpence
into the same white hand.

JACKSON'S CORNER

Somewhere, the sun still shines into Jackson's Corner
and all the dead are alive again
even those I hated, I now love for having been –

a hot afternoon, when the streets are empty
the shops half-day closed,
square functional building seemed squarer,
brick corners sharper
in this country market-town where the youth
of each generation longed to escape
from a town no different than any down the line.

From Jackson's Corner on a clear summer's day
I could look first in one direction – North –
and see my grandparents' house among the park trees
that is now home to a young Polish couple
who have built an extension with an inside toilet,
or – South – to my father's house near the old railway yards –

he choose war – and three streets in
my mother cut the throats of chickens
washing her hands in warm blood and entrails,
like a Roman soothsayer

while five doors down, the stinking bakery
where they broke my back
sandwiched between what is now the carriageway
and the convenience superstore
where my sister sold cheap Taiwan bangles –
she is dead now too, before her allotted years
yet caught between, in the years now steadily advancing
on the still living

Jackson is gone too, I don't remember him,
his sexless mannequins turned to the wall
bemused at suits no longer fashionable
like button and thread cases,
overhead pneumatic tubes shuttling across the room.

And a Twelfth parade passes Jackson's Corner
giving blood to ghosts –
I am only the body borrowed and passed down
by these ancestors who left no trace,
who buried their children with tradition,
conquerors of the neat grass verges
Thiepval, Milltown, Arlington
and all the great deserts of the world.

At Jackson's Corner, the hot wind blows
through from two streets
you could smell the heat from the pavements
the discarded cigarettes, the lollipop sticks,
the yellow rape heads of the girdling fields –
we thought we owned it all

the long afternoon, empty of cars and people
the startled reflections of mannequins caught in the window glass.

Giving Blood to Ghosts: Reading Gary Allen's *Jackson's Corner*

Gary Allen is another poet who addresses disputed territory, mostly with an even less optimistic vision than the one we've just discussed. He was born in Ballymena, County Antrim, in 1959, and is the author of over a dozen collections, beginning in the mid-nineties with the humble UK publisher, K.T. Publications, who printed three of his early pamphlets, before his first full-length collection, *Languages*, appeared in 2002 (Flambard/Black Mountain Press). Allen has travelled widely, working in a variety of jobs across Europe, and his writing reflects this, but his Ulster roots feature heavily in much of his best work, including *Jackson's Corner* (Greenwich Exchange, 2016), which I'll discuss here.

Several commentators note a downbeat tone in Allen's writing, but this might be expected in a poet who deals so often with the 'troubles'. Where Seamus Heaney dug like an archeologist for his metaphors, finding parallels for the troubles in burials and excavations, Allen is more likely to address them directly, as seen in many of the poems I don't have room to include here: in 'Red Bird', for instance, young people are 'shot or stabbed, abducted after the dance' [34], in 'Seen Unseen' 'the seeds of fear' are sown in a world of 'cut throats' [35], and in 'Protestant Dolls' the speaker's sister 'had her face kicked in/up on the playing fields/her Protestant dolls tossed into the storm drain' [56]. In other words Allen's poems are never squeamish about the reality of conflict, and rarely anything other than pessimistic about the causes; but optimism isn't compulsory, and they are a vehicle for what feels like honest rage, mostly untempered by sentimentality.

Where Ní Churreáin's poems exhibit a lean, pared-down aesthetic, Allen's work is the opposite: he has a loose, discursive style, particularly in *Jackson's Corner* where many poems have a narrative focus, frequently taking the form of reminiscences about Ballymena characters. They come to us as vivid, fully-rounded people: 'The Temple Builders', for instance, presents a working-class father who makes 'the manly pilgrimage/from work to pub, from betting-shop, to bed', revealing a world shaped by the inherited narratives of masculinity and religious cant. The speaker recalls helping his father – the ironic Temple Builder – with a DIY project, but the two of them fail in tandem: '"in the name of God," he cursed', as his son tries to assist him. Notice how the religious obscenities provide an ironic counterpoint to the title, and the idea of 'temple building' becomes a figurative edifice of frustration, abuse and bewilderment. In the final line of the poem we're told that his father slips him a 'still-hot silver sixpence' [62], and this is a telling detail: the reward is confusing for the child, of course, coming as it does in a context of failure and abuse; it suggests that the wages of such failure are guilty compensation from a father who, at some deep level, knows he is at fault; he perhaps also feels he knows how the world *should* work – through generosity, kindness, and reward for honest effort.

We find similar contradictions throughout *Jackson's Corner*, not least in the title poem. This builds around the image of Jackson the Tailor, a corner building at a junction in the poet's home town of Ballymena, which teems with harrowing memories for the speaker. It's a town of enduring bigotry and conflict, sustained by traditions 'giving blood to ghosts', where the spoils of battle are meaningless: the victors are merely 'conquerors of the neat grass verges [...] and all the great deserts of the world' [79/80]. Allen's pessimism is clear, but there's also ambivalence in the poem: see for instance the first stanza with his claim that he loves the people he once hated; this ambivalence is developed in more subtle ways as the poem develops, not least via the increasingly nostalgic tone. Notice how the poem is full of deliberate contradictions: spent cigarettes and lollipop sticks conjure notions of transient indulgences, which are at least sweet and satisfying while they last; the image of urban litter is offset by the reference to nature's rape yellow; the idea of emptiness is qualified by the 'we' of companionship; the meagre wares of the shop window are balanced by the fleeting promise of ownership; and while the streets through which the hot wind blows are empty, Allen is grateful for their existence both in reality and memory. He can love them 'for having been', along with the folks who smoked the cigarettes and licked the lollipops. Existence itself is meaningful for Allen, then, and despite its traumas he can't hide his fondness for the 'long afternoon', or help but acknowledge the occasional pleasure he took in them. The book brims with similar tensions, and together the poems combine to conjure a potent sense of place, and a gifted poet's complex and contradictory relationship with it.

How Can Poets Use It?

- Like many of the poets in this book, Allen is good at tapping into the creative energy generated by contradictions. He is drawn to the lived experience, and reading him can help us find ways of addressing the tensions in our own lives, either through metaphor, as in 'The Temple Builders' or textured description, as in 'Jackson's Corner'.

• Allen is adept at delineating character, which is a lot harder in poetry than in prose. He can render characters succinctly, and while he uses broad brushstrokes, he always manages to avoid caricature and stereotype. We can see this in 'The Temple Builders', where character is revealed both directly and indirectly: sometimes he literally tells us what his father was like, but he also shows him via his voice and behaviour. He has a great sense of how to effectively combine showing and telling, and it is worth studying this aspect of his work closely.

Writing Prompts

• Write a poem about trying to build something with your worst enemy. Think carefully about your choice of building, and how the inevitable conflicts between you and your enemy will manifest themselves.

• Much of Allen's work in *Jackson's Corner* is underpinned by contradiction: the tension created by conflicted feelings. All of us are conflicted about something, so try to think of an issue, incident, or character that has created similar conflicts in you, and write a poem about it. Make the poem as place-specific as possible.

• Following Allen's lead in 'Jackson's Corner', think of a building that is in some way representative of a region for you, preferably one that you're very familiar with (perhaps from your hometown). Write a poem about the building: begin by describing it, and then go on to personalise the poem by unpacking the details of your own experience of it.

Slim Volumes in a Similar Vein

If you enjoy Gary Allen's collection you might also like *Streets of Belfast* by Alistair Graham (Lapwing Press, 2012), *Occupational Hazard* by Aidan Hayes (Lapwing Press, 2013), *Three Seasons for Burning* by Lynda Plater (Wayleave, 2016), *Growing up in Colour* by Maurice Devitt (Doire Press, 2018), *Ah Men*, by Simon Lewis (Doire Press, 2019), and *Street Light Amber* by Noel Duffy (Ward Wood Publishing, 2020).

REGIONS II: PLACE AND IDENTITY

The two books I've just discussed ponder inherited conflicts associated with the authors' region of birth, which in both cases is disputed territory: while Ní Churreáin sees a solution of sorts to the disputes she's inherited, Allen remains ambivalent, and largely contents himself with transforming the traumatic past into art. Both offer fascinating insights into the way sensitive minds can respond to the traditions, frustrations and politics of place. Now I'll turn more specifically to the relationship between place and identity, particularly in relation to race and voice.

Anyone familiar with contemporary poetry will know that this is well-charted ground among high-profile poets. Just consider some of the recent winners of the T.S Eliot Poetry Prize: Sarah Howe's *Loop of Jade* (2015), Ocean Vuong's *Night Sky With Exit Wounds* (2017), Roger Robinson's *A Portable Paradise* (2019), and Bhanu Kapil's *How to Wash a Heart* (2020), are all books in which identity and place clash – it is clearly a dominant theme of profound relevance to our culture. Here I'll discuss a lesser-known slim volume that addresses similar conflicts with equal passion and eloquence, Roy McFarlane's *Beginning with Your Last Breath* (2016).

Roy McFarlane *Beginning with Your Last Breath*[35]

PAPERS

The day I was called into my mother's bedroom
the smell of cornmeal porridge still coloured the air,

windowsills full of plants bloomed
and dresses half-done hung from wardrobe doors

and her Singer sewing machine came to rest
like a mail train arriving at its final destination,

foot off the pedal, radio turned down, she beckoned,
touched me with those loving hands.

Shrouded in the softness of light from the net curtains,
her eyes filled with sensitivity, hesitated as she spoke to me,

---

[35] Roy McFarlane, *Beginning with Your Last Breath* (Rugby: Nine Arches Press, 2016). All quotations will be taken from this edition.

sit down son, there's something I need to tell you.

She picked up her heavy Bible with gold-edged leaves,
turning the pages as they whispered and somewhere

in the middle of Psalms she removed a sheet of paper
which read, '*In the matter of the Adoption Act. 1958*'

and I'm lost in the reading of a name of an infant,
sinking into the cream background, falling between the lines.

Only the tenderness of her voice drew me out of the margins;
words fallen now echo through the years.

We adopted you from the age of 6 months,

enveloped by this revelation I couldn't move,
imagined it couldn't be right because I knew my mother;

the aroma of her Morgan pomaded hair, her olive oiled skin,
the Y scarred throat that she hid under buttoned up blouses

and like a hymn I found myself telling her, *it's alright, it's alright.*

NIGHT AND DAY

I learned verses of love with
a beautiful two-tone Rudie,
her tight jeans and t-shirts held
her as intimately as I did in the day time
in between lessons, common room
and the sports hall. We kissed like
lovers from a Klimt painting; our bodies
ablaze with the touch of each other

and we made love in open fields
painting beautiful colours
until the sun went down ...
                          night times
we sneaked out; the daughter
of a single mother and the son
of a preacher man; star-crossed lovers
at the Rising Star or The Molineux
waiting for the healing of Lovers Rock
where bass speakers mesmerised,
locked us together in perfect poetry,
the symmetry of a Rodin sculpture
brought to life on the dance floor
lost in Janet Kaye's 'Silly Games'.

Welcomed With Closed Doors: Reading Roy McFarlane's *Beginning with Your Last Breath*

Roy McFarlane is a former Birmingham Poet Laureate, and those who've read him struggle to understand why he isn't more widely known. It might have something to do with his relatively small output so far: his first collection, *Beginning with Your Last Breath*, didn't appear until he was in his fifties, although this was quickly followed by another fine book, *The Healing Next Time* (2018). As a Poetry Book Society Recommendation, the latter received slightly more attention than the former, although it's his heavily autobiographical debut volume that for me best captures the spirit of McFarlane's voice.

The first poem I've cited here, 'Papers', depicts the day his mother told him he was adopted, and is typical of his expansive, storytelling style. The opening stanzas offer a masterclass in scene-setting, with at least four of the five senses engaged: the smell of porridge, the touch of a hand, the filtered light, and the rattle of a sewing machine coming to rest like a train at the end of the line. The speaker goes on to describe the adoption papers produced from between the pages of a family bible as they 'whispered' their 'revelation'; it continues the biblical imagery at the end, closing with his response to his adoptive mother's news, 'like a hymn I found myself telling her, *it's alright, it's alright*' [11/12]. The poem is heavy on emotion, and adjectives, and it is representative of McFarlane's style in its willingness to flirt with overstatement and sentimentality. What makes it work for me is our sense of the poet's proximity to his subject: throughout the collection we have the impression of a poet operating at the edge of emotion, where subtlety and linguistic refinement take second place to feeling; I think he creates a context in which extremity has legitimacy, and its own rhetorical force. I make this point because it goes against what is often taught in creative writing courses, where students are usually encouraged to deal with emotions in an understated way. On this issue I disagree with the critic in the *Poetry Review* who disparaged McFarlane's book for its 'lack of lexical economy'[36]. The critic offers the following extract from another poem in the collection, 'As I did the night before', as an example of what he deems McFarlane's sloppy writing:

> It was the way you used to put your tights on,
> after a moment of loving
> or at the dawn of a new morning.
> There was nothing more sensual
> or visual than you sitting at the edge of the bed [54]

---

[36] Kayombo Chingonyi, 'No Better Measure', *The Poetry Review*, 107, 1, Spring, 2017, 107-111

We assume that the reviewer – like an overzealous editor – would want to omit the phrase 'used to', or adjust ostensibly tautological phrases like 'dawn of a new morning'. Again this is the kind of advice that is often given on creative writing courses, where less is always felt to be more.[37] Frequently this is true, and poets should usually strive for succinct expression, but is it *always* so? To elide the tautologies in this case would undermine the poem – it would detract from a voice that's made richer and more human by such informality. I said in my introduction that I was interested in 'page' rather than 'performance' poetry, but that doesn't mean that the spirit and rhythms of spoken discourse are always unwelcome on the page.[38] Far from it. I think McFarlane makes informal language work, and for him less isn't *always* more: what at first sight appears bloated, becomes sumptuous and expansive for those readers who are sensitive to spoken forms, and who are willing to adjust their ear accordingly.

As suggested, McFarlane's passions are personal: he's interested in his experience of growing up in the West Midlands, and an

[37] Forrest Wickman argues eloquently against this approach in an article called 'Against Subtlety. It Sucks' where he says that 'bluntness is also a virtue', pointing out that when 'artists don't muffle themselves in the service of subtlety ... they kindle fervour and fire' *Critical Creative Writing: Essential Readings on the Writer's Craft* by Janelle Adsit (ed) (Bloomsbury, 2018): 232

[38] I have occasionally seen reviews that criticise Afro-Caribbean 'page poetry' on similar grounds; indeed, Roger Robinson's T.S. Eliot Prize-winning *A Portable Paradise* was disparaged in the same journal for identical reasons: Robinson's poetry is described as 'circumlocutory', and in need of an editor to take out 'unnecessary' adverbs, repetition, and 'elementary problems of composition' [see Marek Sullivan, 'A Pocket Babel', *The Poetry Review*, 110, 3, Autumn, 2020, 128-132]. I'm more inclined to agree with Bridget Minamore's review of McFarlane, who argues that 'there's a quality about [McFarlane] which makes [her] want to step away from academic language'. By 'academic language' I also take her to mean 'academic' assumptions about the inevitable superiority of linguistic economy [https://poetryschool.com/reviews/review-beginning-last-breath-roy-mcfarlane/]

identity complicated by race, class, and his status as an adopted
son. He has a strong sense of region, as seen in poems like 'Tipton',
which is unfortunately too long to include here in full. 'Tipton' is
a 'tongue-tipping/double syllable of a word' that denotes an area
of the Black Country 'between Brum and Wolves'; here the locals
call him 'bab', and say 'I cor walk past ya without/putting me onds
on ya' [59-60]. McFarlane grew up in the Black Country, and the
region inspires both warmth and bitterness in equal measure. In
'That place just off the M6', for instance, we're told that Black
folks 'felt at home with people/who couldn't speak the Queen's
English', and he sees Wolverhampton's statue of Lady Wulfruna
as a West Midlands 'Statue of Liberty/welcoming the poor and the
needy'; however, he also notes how Black people were too often
'welcomed with closed doors, cold looks and biting words' [21-
22]. Local hostility toward the immigrant community is frequently
a source of anger, expressed powerfully in poems like 'After all is
said and done' which details his friend, Bevan's, suffering from
racial violence: it sees him 'beaten and bleeding' in front of St Peter's
Church in Wolverhampton, while 'Christ looks down helplessly
nailed to his cross'. We're told that while Bevan 'stopped calling
on Jesus', he nevertheless 'still believed' [34-35], and we sense that
McFarlane still believes too: despite justified anger at the
consequences of prejudice, there is a possibility of happiness and
redemption with friends, lovers, and family. In 'Surrender to the
air', for instance, he reflects on his time playing basketball with
Bevan, 'and the launch into the air/defying gravity':

> We glided knowing that we were beauty in motion,
> bodies elite, that when we released

> that ball
> after the double pump ...

> we had surrendered to the air. [36-37]

The basketball court is an environment of freedom in a world of discrimination and violence; here, at last, their bodies become beautiful and 'elite' rather than a source of hatred. Moments of freedom and transcendence with lovers are also numerous, as at the end of 'Night and Day', which I've quoted in full above. It's a poem about being young in the Black Country, and has a delightfully joyous feel. The high art allusions in this poem are never in danger of being pretentious, qualified as they are by low culture references – 'star-crossed lovers/at the Rising Star' [29] alludes simultaneously to Shakespeare and a Bilston strip club. This and other pop culture references suggest a specific historical moment, locating the action in time and place. However, it is significant that, despite being historically and geographically grounded, 'symmetry', perfection and 'life' for the speaker are associated with the experience of being 'lost' (albeit 'in Janet Kaye's "Silly Games"'): we get the impression that happiness for a black man in the Black Country necessitates such moments of escape and disengagement: it's not so much 'place' that is celebrated here, then, but the compensations offered by that place, which in this case involves music and, above all, the 'perfect poetry' of love and sex. What particularly appeals to me is the tone of the poem, which is both uninhibited and enraptured, suggestive of a speaker who is unashamedly savouring the moment. Once more it treads a fine line between art and excess, but again McFarlane gets it right.

How Can Poets Use It?

• I'd recommend that poets read McFarlane because he demonstrates that it's possible to break some of the rules regarding economy and restraint in poetry. His is a muscular, sensuous voice, shaped by region, and that shaping has created a conscious artlessness which has eloquence, candour, poignancy, and resonance because of, rather than in spite of, its excesses.

• McFarlane's work has a colloquial feel that stems not just from his occasional use of dialect, but from his willingness to embrace his region as a subject, and his ability to identify the specific incidents and conflicts that will be of interest to others. Like all good regional writers he deals in relevant specifics.

Writing Prompts

• McFarlane's poems often work because we get a sense of a passion that is unmediated by too much polish and refinement. Try to write a poem about something or someone you love which addresses the subject in a similarly unfettered way. Use adjectives to celebrate your emotions, rather than trying to eschew or impose control on them; don't be vague about your emotions, link them to specific details as McFarlane does, but don't be embarrassed to enthuse. Perhaps imagine that you are trying to convince someone about the intensity of your passion, rather than trying to write a poem about it.

• While poems about place are often about community and belonging, they can also be about alienation. Try to imagine what it's like to feel like an outsider in a community that, for whatever reason, is hostile to you – write a poem about how this might affect your concept of 'home'.

Slim Volumes in a Similar Vein

If you enjoy this book's themes you might also enjoy *Letters Home* by Jennifer Wong (Nine Arches Press, 2020), and *Road Trip* by Marvin Thompson (Peepal Tree Press, 2020). Other collections about identity based conflict with a West Midlands focus include Rupinder Kaur's *Rooh* (Verve, 2018), Nafeesa Hamid's *Besharam* (Verve, 2018) and Amerah Saleh's *I Am Not From Here* (Verve, 2018).

REGIONS III: PLACE AND DIALECT

Until recently using dialect in poems might have been deemed a brave thing to do: as Ben Wilkinson said, 'regional English accents tend to receive short shrift, if not outright mockery' from the poetry establishment[39]. The Black Country dialect in particular is one of the least prestigious in the UK, but West Midlands poet Liz Berry has done much to reveal its poetic potential in recent years: her award winning collections *Black Country* (2014) and *The Republic of Motherhood* (2016), draw heavily on the vernacular, and have

---

[39] Ben Wilkinson, '*Black Country* by Liz Berry poetry review – "love flowed out of me like honey"', *The Guardian*, November, 2014. https://www.theguardian.com/books/2014/nov/21/black-country-liz-berry-review-poetry-collection

helped position this maligned dialect in the realm of high culture. Berry manages to avoid the temptations of parody and sentimentality that often mar regional verse; she exploits the subtly subversive potential of dialect, exploring voice and identity in ways that are both visceral and intellectually engaged. An emerging writer who occupies similar territory is the Dudley-born R.M. Francis, whose first full collection, *Subsidence*, appeared in 2020.

R.M. Francis's *Subsidence*[40]

SLEEPIN' BEASTS

Skies mirror coal seams and slate of cinder smoke –
tethers grey birds to its oil slick,
cloaks wenches' washing lines,
hanging out failed whites
for blokes on the box
who doh know how to clear
the cloud in their eyes.

Down on The Wrenner land is littered –
winds clip used cans through estates,
passed scorched out sofas weedy teens
use to toll the day.
This land –
nesting tumour in a cold parish.

Iss like our Tim keeps cantin':
weem cut from 'ere in all iss umber,

---

[40] R.M. Francis, *Subsidence* (Ripon: Smokestack Books, 2020). All quotations will be taken from this edition.

like the cut was cut from clay.
We ay nature's sons,
just med of it, someway.
'Cause weem cut that way,
weem cut away.

Down on The Wrenner air is soiled
with unwashed pets, cigarettes,
dried booze, pizza crust breath.
This air –
pricked silica leak of rotting cells.

Tim treds the towpath to 'is ESA review,
over grit and sand 'e used to alchemy to glass
but now just plays a part
in weathering muck.

They doh know
wass under theya –
our earth's rotten
with trilobites.
Weem stompin' on sleepin' beasts.

BORDERLANDS
'We're all Middle Class now!'

Lord Prescott

It's always been the borderlands –
borders we make, borders
put upon us
borders in the borders.

Granddad holds forth about Kuala Lumpur conquests
we've heard again and again. Nan does her duty.

Old coals built them and their difference.

Stambermill viaduct divides his growth:
site of tissue bombs and resin bongs,
graffiti wars between Baggies and Wolves.
Looming grey bricks arch over plains
where the Stour cuts industrial estates
and municipal grasses where the kids,
whose Dads were on the box after Kuwait,
taught us porn and fags and illicit words.
We weren't quite as *working* as them –
didn't matter then.

Paul moved south after Uni, *e' sez charnce and barth now,*
Linda told 'im – there ay an R in it, chance rhymes with pants.

Old coals burn in tongues.

The middle son boards
with Mother, she could tell a tale –
the only child of a factory wench
and ex-guardsman,
with council estate maisonette,
the stench of salted meats
and carbolic soap. Father,
eldest of three in Post-War Semi,
where tobacco, wine and classical
music steep the scene.
Watched his Mum die at seventeen,
never says a word about it.

Old coals, still subsiding.

Their spawn, treading waters.
Working enough for Pennfields,
Middle enough for Pedmore –
he ploughed a border. *Nah, 'e's alright,*
'e knows Armitage but 'e'll gerr'on
the end of a cross with a minute of lunch
to spare.

 Madge,
 who did her Tony Harrison thing,
 said *a bit of honest vulgarity, better*
 than them imagined pretentions.

  Old coal gets a spit polish.

New builds and period homes mottled
the other side of Stambermill, where the wraith
of the viaduct is fogged. A grinning
perjurer declares *things can only get better.*

 I doh like 'im, Nan says, *'e's an hyena.*
 'Er was right.

  Old coal, old oil, old game.
We had books,
Dad subscribed to Reader's Digest
and demolished lit for fun –
a big American firm took him on.
Mum had her trinkets –
corn dollies, porcelain mice –
cultured a supermarket into a classroom.

They had rows of Penguin books,
neatly aligned amongst black and white
family portraits and kitchens

of locally sourced goods.
Have you ever been anywhere outside Europe?
We weren't quite as *Middle* as them,
we noticed that then.

Cut That Way: Reading R.M. Francis's *Subsidence*

R.M. Francis is interested in how Black Country identity is created, and the disparate things that contribute to one's sense of self, including geography, history, and language. You'll notice that the opening stanza of 'Sleepin' beasts' paints a bleak picture of the region: words like 'tethers' suggest entrapment, and the 'wenches' of the Black Country struggle in vain to cleanse the stain they've inherited; their 'blokes on the box' suffer a sickness they can neither shake nor fathom, a chronic 'cloud in their eyes'. But, as with Gary Allen, there are compensations too, particularly in the spirit of belonging that often features in Francis's work. The poem goes on to reveal how the region shapes its people ('*weem cut from 'ere in all iss umber*'): according to this character, Black Country people *are* the region, inseparable from it; just as the region's canals (cuts) were 'cut from' local clay, so the people are 'cut that way'. The idea of a connection between people and place is extended to include a sense of belonging within the community, implied here by the phrase 'our Tim', emphasising blood ties and connections of a human kind.

Like several of his poems, 'Sleepin' Beasts' focuses on a very specific place – an area near Dudley called Wren's Nest, which is built on land rich in fossils, together with the legacy of industry, quarrying and mining (the geological consequences of which give rise to his book's title, *Subsidence*). There's a clear awareness of this history, particularly in the final stanza, where the speaker says explicitly, '*Weem stompin' on sleepin' beasts*' [37/8]. The idea of 'sleepin'' fossils suggests a past that cannot be forgotten, or escaped: local folk must acknowledge their connection to the things that precede and underpin them; and they must tread lightly and respectfully for fear of subsidence. Thus Black Country heritage is complex, dark, inescapable, and potentially turbulent: the land may literally consume its people!

Dialect has the potential to help sustain traditions and community connections for Francis: in poems like 'Burning Tongues' (not included in full here), he refers to the vernacular as 'the burn': dialect has the power to 'burn back' on authority and the mainstream, which is negatively associated with Received Pronunciation, and 'ministers/of education immersed in/double spayke' [11]. It's worth noting that, unlike Liz Berry, Francis chooses not to include a dialect glossary in the book, a decision that I think augments its political edge – certainly it enhances our sense of the region's difference, and what Francis sees as its socio-cultural estrangement. While political sentiments are generally felt rather than seen in *Subsidence*, they become evident in poems like 'Borderlands', which is one of my favourite poems in the book, hence my decision to include it in full. It opens with Lord Prescott's contention that '*We're all Middle Class now!*', and strongly contests this notion. Referring to his Black Country ancestors, Francis tells us that 'Old coals built them and their difference', and it's a difference that persists, ingrained in the psyche and the dialect, reminding us again that 'Old coals burn in tongues'. The 'burn back' against authority is inherent in regional speech, and in the mindset shaped by class distinctions that the community can't forget, made explicit in the final stanza by lines like 'Old coal, old oil, old game' [31]. 'Borderlands' is another poem in which the fossils of the past bear heavily on the present; the 'old coal' defines the Black Country – it's the fuel that fired the furnaces, mined from the honeycombed subsiding landscape; it shapes the region and its people just as another fossil fuel (oil) defines the 'old game' of the powers-that-be. Nothing much changes for 'Nan', who feels that Tony Blair's 'hyena' politics give lie to the contention that '*We're all Middle Class now!*' In this poem he explores national politics in a domestic context, then, and we feel its impact at the human level.

Despite its political implications, *Subsidence* offers more than a simple Us and Them dichotomy, and Francis is careful not to overly romanticise the region or its people. We're not allowed to forget that the 'commonsense' mindset shaping Nan's assessment of Tony Blair can also spawn insular and reactionary thinking. For instance, racial conflict is very much part of the Black Country experience, and Francis addresses it in poems like 'Versus', which is sadly too long to include in full here. In this poem the speaker remembers watching a local football game with his uncle; one fellow spectator remarks:

> *That darky can run, cor 'e?*
> Eyes roll, lips stay shut –
> *Bernie doh know better*
> *besides, in 'is own way*
> *'e's bein' nice.*
> *See at fourteen,*
> *mah mate Syed,*
> *a 'paki' from Lye*

was smart and tough
and stuck up for me an' Ash
and ' e played wing at lunch
' cause ' e ' ad a left foot on ' im,
but by sixteen, ' is colour and mine
were too much for ' im
and the others
who learned to be versus

I'm still not sure
eighteen years on,
if I should be cross [21-22]

The stanza beginning 'I'm still not sure' becomes a refrain running through this long poem which uses football as a metaphor for conflicts born of prejudice in a community where people too readily learn to be 'versus'. Regionality can both bind and divide us, then, and Francis's willingness to acknowledge this is one of the many things that distinguishes this sharp and authentic slim volume.

How Can Poets Use It?

• Francis demonstrates how effective the vernacular can be when rendered with skill, and shows how we might use it, not only to achieve a sense of place and character, but also to create and explore cultural and political tensions. He manages to convey the spirit of dialect without resorting to exaggeration or parody – he rarely uses it for comic effect; rather his dialect reveals the dignity of the people who use it, and the surprising lyricism and poignancy of their discourse.

• Francis is excellent at combining dialect with standard English; he manages to weave the former into the latter in ways that add force to the vernacular. Notice how he brackets off the latter with italics when a character is speaking, but also how often dialect and standard English merge in the voice of the poet/speaker, as in the line 'Iss like our Tim keeps cantin''. This merging is effective and important, breaking down the potential hierarchy between standard and colloquial forms of the language.

Writing Prompts

• Create an argument between someone speaking in dialect and someone using RP (Received Pronunciation). Notice how issues of class seem to become a feature of the argument, and how the dialect voice feels transgressive in relation to RP. Can you find a way of using that transgression to drive the poem in a similar way to Francis in 'Borderlands'?

• Taking your lead from 'Sleepin' Beasts', research the history of the region in which you live and think of something significant that could be buried there. Write a poem in which you try to explain the relevance of that artefact to the townsfolk who walk above it every day.

• Take a quote by a politician and write a poem about something you've experienced in your region that seems to contradict it.

• Take a poem that you have written and rewrite it in dialect

– note how it changes the whole character and complexion of the poem; sometimes it can transform a mediocre poem into a much more interesting piece.

Slim Volumes in a Similar Vein

If you enjoy *Subsidence* you might also look at *Soil* by Tim Cresswell (Penned in the Margins, 2013), *Mapping the Moor* by Keith Howden (Penniless Press, 2019), *Alice and the North* by Anne Caldwell (Valley Press, 2020). Those particularly interested in West Midlands and dialect poetry might enjoy *Urban Dawn* by Brendan Hawthorne (Bluechrome, 2004) and *Close* by Emma Purshouse (Offa's Press, 2018).

HIGHBROW, LOWBROW AND NOBROW: THE JOY OF ACCESSIBILITY

If there's one thing that connects our two most recent poet laureates in the UK it's their combination of what Robert Lowell described as 'the raw and the cooked': their winning amalgam of cultural sophistication and the common touch. As Lisa Allardice said of Simon Armitage, 'His wit, grit and gift for mixing the demotic with the metaphorical have long made him the people's poet'; neither highbrow nor lowbrow, he describes himself as 'nobrow'[41]. Similarly it was Carol Ann Duffy's tendency to close the gap between high and low that led Geoffrey Hill – a longstanding champion of 'difficult' poetry – to compare her to a 'Mills and Boon' writer[42].

Armitage and Duffy share their nobrow status with some of the

English speaking world's most popular poets, of course, including the likes of Billy Collins, Wendy Cope, Roger McGough, and numerous others; writers in this category tend to have a preference for plain diction, a flair for popular humour, and a knack for avoiding grandiosity and intellectualism. There are countless collections I could use to illustrate this spirit of accessibility in more detail, but I've opted for Maggie Butt's *Lipstick* and Robert Etty's *Planes Flying Over.*

Maggie Butt, *Lipstick*[43]

TUMBLING

The weeks are tumbling over one another
over and over like Chinese acrobats:
impossible handsprings, effortless,
tinsel-dressed, bright with sequins
spangles and greasepaint and sweat
somersaulting so fast they are blurred
until you can't see where one starts and
another finishes, tumbling out of the circus tent
on and on, up the dusty hillside road
off to the horizon.

---

[41] Lisa Allardice, 'Interview with Simon Armitage', *The Guardian*, 2019, https://www.theguardian.com/books/2019/jun/07/simon-armitage-poet-laureate-ted-hughes-came-from-the-next-valley

[42] See Alison Flood, 'Carol Ann Duffy is "wrong" about poetry, says Geoffrey Hill', *The Guardian*, 2012, https://www.theguardian.com/books/2012/jan/31/carol-ann-duffy-oxford-professory-poetry

[43] Maggie Butt, *Lipstick* (London: Greenwich Exchange Publishing, 2007). All quotations will be taken from this edition.

LIPSTICK

In wartime women turn to red
swivel-up scarlet and carmine
not in solidarity with spilt blood
but as a badge of beating hearts.

This crimson is the shade of poets
silenced for speaking against torture,
this vermilion is art
surviving solitary confinement,

this cerise defies the falling bombs
the snipers taking aim at bread-queues,
this ruby's the resilience of girls
who tango in the pale-lipped face of death.

ON MY 85TH BIRTHDAY

For breakfast there will be chocolate,
heaped and glossy like a race-horse,
sweating with saturated fat.

And I will devour it,
cramming in the melting mouthfuls
coating my fingers and my face.

In the morning I'll ride a motorbike
black leathers and no helmet
white hair streaming loose, a challenge.

For lunch there will be crispy bacon
in white bread, with butter,
mouthwatering aroma of defiance.

After my nap in the bed-shop window;

I will invite my doctor in for scones,
and lick thick clotted cream along the knife.

And in the sunset
I will ascend to heaven in a glider
singing in the eerie silence.

The next day I'll dance barefoot in the rain
or take up smoking (inhaling deeply)
or sub-aqua diving,
or run with scissors

if I choose.

STAR-LIT

Laughing home barefoot from the disco
star-lit, care-free, safe within the pack
high heels dangling from our hands like bracelets,
cold pavements salve dance-blistered toes,
the pulse of living sings along our blood.
We are reflected in dark High Street windows
so the night is full of us, our youth.
The cars are few, our voices own the air,
and you three boys stride out, long-limbed,
the world laid out before you for the taking,
throw back your heads, cry to the moon,
We are gods!
And I look
And you are.

Crimson is the Shade of Poets: Reading Maggie Butt's *Lipstick*

Maggie Butt's first pamphlet, *Quintana Roo*, appeared in 2003, followed by her first full collection, *Lipstick*, published by Greenwich Exchange in 2007. In the latter, Butt's intelligibility, humour, and optimism create a tone that appeals to me, and her thematically diverse poems are characterised by a delightfully upbeat, user-friendly take on the world that certainly qualifies her as a 'nobrow' poet as I've defined it above. Notice how, in 'Tumbling', Butt deals with the potentially negative themes of transience and turmoil, but manages to offset pessimism with humour. The light, buoyant tone that's created by the rather incongruous 'acrobats' image is typical, and we discern a strong sense of joy in the spectacle as the poem develops [35]. It reflects the spirit of the book as a whole: while Butt's subject matter is frequently dark, the buoyancy persists, and her treatment almost always has a positive and redemptive feel.

I enjoy the note of feminine defiance that frequently accompanies this positive energy, as in the title poem of *Lipstick*, quoted above. Lavinia Greenlaw once said that 'a poem should be arranged so that, once inside it, you can see everywhere at once'[44], and I feel that's the case here: once we understand what red lipstick means for Butt, we see 'everywhere at once'. For instance, the distinction between red as the colour of life ('beating hearts') and the red of battlefield death ('spilt blood') offers a simple and striking antithesis, but the fact that it's gendered via lipstick illuminates the whole: we understand that women are in solidarity exclusively

[44] W.N. Herbert, Matthew Hollis (eds), *Strong Words: Modern Poets on Modern Poetry* (Bloodaxe, 2000), 274

with the former – survival resides with them, and their 'scarlet', 'crimson', and 'ruby' denote life 'in the pale-lipped face of death'. Again, the tone remains light despite the dark theme – the references to cosmetics and dancing are humorously at odds with the subject; it also reclaims the way make-up signifies in patriarchy, where it's often disparaged as the mark of a fallen woman, particularly in the case of 'scarlet'.

This note of feminine resistance is sounded throughout Butt's work, as in the nine-line poem 'Small', which I haven't included in full, but which also makes a case for passive rebellion; it references the bloodless Carnation Revolution which overthrew Portugal's Estado Novo in 1974, and it closes:

> Let me be a Lisbon flower girl
> who slips a fresh carnation in the barrel
> of a gun, and blooms a revolution. [19]

For Butt, the fallen world is redeemable via feminine intervention, and I love the image she employs to convey this notion: she amplifies its force deftly with the word 'blooms', giving her flower girl's pacifism its subversive potency.

Another subversive character is the heroine of 'On my 85th Birthday', one of the more overtly comic poems in this book. Here the octogenarian speaker lists a series of reckless acts, from eating too much chocolate to riding a motorbike without a crash helmet, concluding with a reference to 'sub-aqua diving' and running with scissors [27]. As images of rebellion go, these are rather tame stock gestures, but this is deliberate, I think, and in keeping with Butt's simple, direct style; also the humour here creates a degree of self-awareness that saves the poem from cliché. The important line is the final one, 'if I choose', reflecting the sense of entitlement and independence that informs much of her writing.

What I particularly like about Butt's work is that she extends her assertion of freedom and independence to other genders. This can be seen in 'Star-Lit', another poem where humour serves an important function, creating a playful context for a reflection on the male ego. We might wonder if the speaker really thinks of the young men as 'gods', or if she is being ironic; for me the tone is clearly and typically celebratory rather than condemnatory: she is sanguine about their youthful excess, applauding their sense of limitless potential along with her own. She doesn't mock their 'cry to the moon': she is willing to accommodate it in the spirit of human optimism and ebullience. The final line, 'And you are' [29] is a gloriously unequivocal exclamation, and coming from a female perspective there's a sense in which it reclaims masculinity in ways that a male voice couldn't: in Butt's poem testosterone-fuelled exuberance is equated with her own youthful energy, suggesting that the 'pulse of living' animates and unites us as human beings, regardless of gender.

These poems exemplify the spirit of so-called 'nobrow' as I see it: they are simple poems, but far from simplistic. They are politically engaged, but decidedly non-partisan; serious, but simultaneously light. Among other things, Butt brings her unpretentious touch to bear on the complex issue of gender signification, interrogating our assumptions with plain discourse; she employs humour that invites us into the subject, displaying a rare talent that distinguishes her from many of her highbrow and lowbrow contemporaries.

How Can Poets Use It?

• I think poets could learn a lot from Butt's understated humour. Humour is a powerful rhetorical device, and one that is well worth cultivating. We all have the capacity for humour (it would be a struggle to get through life without one), and Butt shows us how humour can offer a useful way of dealing with difficult issues like war, aging, and gender politics. Butt's is a popular humour, mostly lacking the acerbic edge of, say, Graham Fulton; it's rarely satirical or hostile, suggesting instead an attitude of forbearance and optimism. It's the kind of humour that invites readers to share her view, rather than implicitly criticising them for disagreeing with it. Importantly, however, Butt's non-threatening tone doesn't suggest acquiescence or quietism – on the contrary, it gives her work force, and a potential popular appeal. In this sense she shows us another way into political issues: her treatment of subjects like war and gender politics are disarming, both in their simplicity and their ostensible equanimity.

Writing Prompts

• Try to find a humorous metaphor for something traumatic, like war, death, or gender oppression. Write a poem based around that metaphor which employs a light tone, exploring the possibilities of the contrasts this creates.

• Write a poem about the outrageous things you'd like to do on your 85th birthday (if you are already 85, go for your 86th). Use exaggeration to augment the comic effect, but ensure that the things you aspire to do in some way reflect your personality, and your values.

• Write a poem that addresses a form of human behaviour that you dislike, such as speaking with one's mouth full, or wearing white socks with a black suit. Think of as many positive things as possible about your chosen annoyance and explore the contrasts they create, exploiting them for humour where possible.

Slim Volumes in a Similar Vein

If you enjoy *Lipstick* then you might also like *How to Dismantle a Hotel Room* by Roz Goddard (Coal Press Publishing, 2006). *Love What is Mortal: Selected Poems* by Norman Schwenk (Parthian, 2016), *Sunbathing on Tyrone Power's Grave* by Kim Powers (Red Hen Press, 2019), *The Significance of a Dress* by Emma Lee (Arachne Press, 2020), *Dressing for the Afterlife* by Maria Taylor (Nine Arches Press, 2020), *Herd Queen* by Di Slaney (Valley Press, 2020), *Greedy Cow* by Fiona Sinclair (Smokestack, 2021)

Robert Etty's *Planes Flying Over*[45]

A WOMAN WALKING

If you see her at all, you'll see her here,
where daffodils line the long road today
from the pink-pantiled house as far as the pond
in the dip at the end, in bloom again
despite the winds that rattle hedges
and scrape the bare fields. She returns

also, week after week, walking neither
slow nor fast, looking down but ahead,
never stepping aside when a car appears
but keeping a practised distance.

The ghost of the thought of a ghost vanishes:
a ghost might materialise out of mist
but not with an Aldi bag for life.
This is her time to walk to the village –
the same time as yours to leave it behind
and drive up this road and past the pond
on your way to where you're going.
Where she's come from you're never aware,
nor whether, it dawned on you one of the weeks,
her destination's actually the village

or the black bush where a buzzard's perched,
the stile to the path to the church that's locked,
the bus stop the bus doesn't stop at now
or a place where she'll pause and turn back.
Before she's ignored you, you steer to the middle,
given that she's no business of yours. In that case
not many people are, and you're no one else's,
except for a few, which means it's a lonely
no one's business, and not surprising
she's walking here with a bag for life on her arm.

NEXT MAY

The folding garden furniture we've kept outside
since May's back in the loft. Please note:

---

[45] Robert Etty, *Planes Flying Over* (Nottingham: Shoestring Books, 2020). All quotations will be taken from this edition.

the legs on both the table and chairs
can close like scissors and nip your fingers,
so I've tied them tightly with binder twine.
The sleeve nuts, four bolts and the Allen keys
are in a self-seal bag in the drawer.
The flowery cover's also in the loft,
washed clean. (Well, maybe not what you'd call clean).

This won't apply till May next year. I mean,
I'll clearly be around to set it up,
but you might want to start if I've gone out.
The other things you'll do better than I would.
It's just I was thinking about your hands.

PLANES FLYING OVER

In my aircraft phase I'd lie on my back
in the neighbours' dandeliony grass
(we shared a path between our gardens)
and scour skies the blues of Humbrol paint lids
for the floating delta or quick, silver cross
of a Meteor, Javelin, Canberra, Lightning,
any V-bomber or anything else
on the flightpath to or from RAF Binbrook,
which even by country bus wasn't far.

Often in summer after a meal
my dad would come down without his jacket,
bringing some stale crust or bacon rind,
and sit on the bench against the nest box
and watch his black hens in the run. He'd say,
'Never mind aeroplanes – chuck some bread in',
and break me a piece to slot through the wire,
and the hens would scuttle over and peck it,
fling it into the air and bicker.

I'd lean beside him and feel his warm shirt
and join in watching the hens. When they'd gulped down
the bread or rind they'd go back to scratting
at the bald earth, scraping for worms or shoots
that weren't there, stabbing between their claws.

Their squawks, clucks and warbles explained, if we
listened, the pointlessness of searching again,
and apologised, but they couldn't help it.
I'm listening now, and they're still explaining
how these days you need to keep doing and trying
because if you stop there'll be nothing.
There they are, under a wide sky near Binbrook,
scratting the same few square yards.

If You Stop There'll Be Nothing: Reading Robert Etty's *Planes Flying Over*

Another nobrow candidate is Lincolnshire-born Robert Etty. A schoolteacher by profession, Etty has been publishing poems since the 80s. Again, straightforward diction and humour characterise his work, but, as with Maggie Butt, his accessibility is accompanied by understated wisdom. His 2020 collection, *Planes Flying Over* is typical of his mature writing, which has seen some development over the years: while he's always favoured rural themes, he has moved increasingly from a painterly approach, with a fondness for static scenes and images, to a more narrative style, with an emphasis on story; as he says in a 2011 interview:

> The rural element is still there to some extent, but there has been a shift in how I treat it. This has occurred in form and language, and in the way rural themes are addressed in a poem. Perhaps now I try

less to 'paint', and I find poems coming more from ideas and small narratives than from scenes.[46]

A typical modern Etty poem will describe an everyday experience, such as losing a scarf, or being stuck behind an annoying woman in a queue, and then gently invite us to consider its potential significance. Sometimes he does this in a final stanza, or even a single line at the end of a poem. In 'A Woman Walking', for instance, he describes a woman who's often seen walking through a village, but no one knows her, or her destination. She keeps 'a practised distance' [49] from people, and they from her. It's partly a poem about people's tendency to keep themselves to themselves; the final image of her 'with a bag for life on her arm' implies that this is a way of life for her, and perhaps for others too: the second person ('you' and 'yours') implicates us in the poem, making us conscious of our own attitudes to others, and suggesting how life can be a 'lonely' business for everyone. But while there's a degree of sadness to this, we don't necessarily see her standoffishness as pernicious, or a symptom of modern alienation; for me the humour implies that it's a benign human trait, and that some of us prefer it this way – human beings often enjoy minding their own business.

Etty's ability to find profundity in the ostensibly commonplace often reminds me of the American nobrow Billy Collins, while his gently mischievous wit is sometimes reminiscent of Wendy Cope. 'Next May', for instance, reads like a note to a spouse, written after an argument about garden furniture. Many will identify with the tone of this domestic situation: they appear to be a couple grown

---

[46] Nicholas Beaumont, 'A look at Lincolnshire's living poets', *The Lincolnite*, August 17, 2011, https://thelincolnite.co.uk/2011/08/a-look-at-lincolnshires-living-poets/

impatient with one another – he of her fussiness, perhaps, she of his untidiness, or procrastination. The scrupulousness with which the speaker has packed everything away suggests that he's making a point, as do the sarcastic references to her assumed superiority. But the joy of the poem resides in the final line, and its reference back to the scissor-like legs that might nip her fingers. Is he genuinely trying to protect her, or is he striving to get the passive-aggressive final word? We assume the latter. It's a poem that, like 'A Woman Walking', hints at a whole way of life: a relationship dogged by inevitable domestic conflicts and annoyances that will nevertheless survive the winter. We're in no doubt that they'll be together next May because the tone of the poem suggests it: the speaker's humour has the feel of a social lubricant, framing frustrations in a way which ameliorates their potential for terminal offence. We're inclined to assume that this is also the tone of their marriage, which will endure, albeit in the fashion of Basil and Sybil Fawlty.

Sometimes Etty's narratives can take the form of reminiscences, as in the title poem of the collection where the speaker returns to his childhood. At the beginning we see him as a child staring up at the skies in search of aircraft – the reference to the 'Humbrol paint lids' locates the perspective in his boyhood, Humbrol being a brand of paint used by model makers; it's a typically well chosen detail that helps us identify with his adolescent point-of-view, adding substance to our sense of his 'aircraft phase' [30], which included making model planes as well as spotting them. It's partly a poem about daydreaming, as we learn when he is joined by his father. His father brings him down to earth with a delightfully colloquial line: 'Never mind aeroplanes – chuck some bread in'. The idiomatic feel of the sentence helps us hear it in our mind; as adults we can identify with his father's no-nonsense sentiments and insistence on practicalities, and in one sense his son can too: certainly he's happy to 'join in', taking his father's advice. The speaker's love and respect for him is clear, and the tone of the piece is affectionate. However, the poem qualifies this a little in the final stanza, where Etty develops the chicken imagery and ponders its meaning. At the close we're reminded that hens, unlike the planes, can't fly, and the speaker is returned to earth in this sense too; yet importantly the message that stays with him doesn't come from his father, but from the hens. While there's a 'pointlessness' to their 'scraping for worms or shoots that weren't there', they persist in 'scratting the same few square yards', because, we assume, the alternative is to do nothing; worse, the alternative is to accept that there *is* nothing, and to accept 'pointlessness' as a way of life ('if you stop there'll be nothing'). In this sense it becomes a poem about purpose, and the closing lines slyly defend his own daydreaming: it gives a point to 'pointlessness', reclaiming his daydreaming as a creative activity. The shift to the present tense at the close suggests that, while plane spotting was merely a 'phase', the hens' lesson endures.

How Can Poets Use It?

• Etty is a master in turning anecdotes into art, and he is worth careful scrutiny for this reason. He sees significance in the everyday, and is adept at fluently and concisely unpacking it. He treats the ostensibly trivial as if it's important, but this rarely involves exaggeration, or straining for effect. Just the opposite. Where hyperbole is usually a staple of comedy, Etty's measured humour is largely created by irony, or the subtle delineation of eccentricity.

• Etty's unpretentious tone is worth studying. There is an appealing patina of informality about his work – his language feels natural, as if the force of his personality is present in the poems, and hasn't been polished out.

Writing Prompts

• Think of the trivial activities that you do in the course of your day, like driving to work, or making a cup of tea. Have there been any occasions on which this was different or disrupted? Even very minor variations to routine can be interesting, and are often better than major incidents. Write a poem that describes that incident, and which amplifies the potential significance of the change in routine. For instance, is there something about the disruption to the routine that illuminates the routine itself?

• Reread 'Bag For Life' and think about the people you know and their relationship with material things. For instance, they might favour a particular style of clothing, carry a lucky charm, or drink from a specific mug. Such associations often inform our perception of such characters – our sense of who they are. Write a poem focusing on the relationship between the character and the object you associate with them, reflecting as far as you can on what the object reveals about them in particular, and perhaps on the human condition in general.

• Reread 'Planes Flying Over' and think of any encounters you've had with animals in your life, either positive or negative. Again, it doesn't matter how trivial (it's hard to think of anything more trivial than Etty's hens). The fact that you have remembered the encounter at all is probably significant, so spend some time reflecting on why it's stuck in your mind. Write a poem that strives to explain the endurance of that memory.

Slim Volumes in a Similar Vein

If you like *Planes Flying Over* you might also try *Early Train* by Jonathan Davidson (Smith/Doorstop, 2011), *My Family and Other Superheroes* by Jonathan Edwards (Seren, 2014), *Voicings* by Bill Dodd (Spring Onion Press, 2018), *The Goldsmith's Apprentice* by Keith Chandler (Fair Acre Press, 2018), *Elastic Man* by Paul McGrane (Indigo Dreams, 2018), *Yes But What Is This? What Exactly?* by Ian McMillan (Smith/Doorstop, 2020), *The Human Heart* by Hugh Underhill (Shoestring, 2020), *Fix* by Miles Salter (Winter & May, 2020), *Borrowed Light* by Ken Haas (Red Mountain Press, 2020), and *Paper Cut* by Hamish Whyte (Shoestring Press, 2020).

DEATH AND THE LIVED EXPERIENCE

Mortality is a common theme in poetry, as it is in the arts generally. As with anything that generates powerful emotions, death is hard to write about from a personal perspective. Poets can learn a lot from reading those who write well about their experience of bereavement, or the reality of their own mortality. For me, stand out collections in recent years include Denise Riley's *Say Something Back* (2016) and Helen Dunmore's *Inside the Wave* (2017): the former deals with the death of the author's son in ways that redefine elegy as a genre, while the latter's reflections on mortality create exquisite metaphors for life in the face of death. I learned a lot from both of them, but I also learned much from two less well-known slim volumes that explore similar territory with equal originality and courage: Carole Coates's *When the Swimming Pool Fell into the Sea* (2021) and Sean Elliott's *Poems: 1998-2016* (2020).

Carole Coates's *When the Swimming Pool Fell into the Sea*[47]

CRAZY DAYS 1

How many beds you say
How many beds have we slept in?

now that you remember I sleep elsewhere
and like redbush tea in the morning
but you can't remember why I left the big bed
in the crazy days
when you cried out about the hole, the great pit
in the bed, scrambling out of the way for fear of falling.
You could feel the sharp edge of it
smell the cold airs drifting up
so we changed places but you worried that I would fall
down the chasm you'd discovered so I went away

---

[47] Carole Coates, *When the Swimming Pool Fell into the Sea* (Nottingham: Shoestring Press, 2021). All quotations will be taken from this edition.

to the attic bedroom

and thought about, though you could not, our first bed –
under the window that looked to the orchard
and I knelt on the bed and watched you walking
among apple trees in an autumn so still that the leaves
hung quiet as fruit and you cupped your hand
round a small brown russet but did not pick it
because you always kept all the rules
as if it would help, as if it would do you good.

Now the chasm is closing and you come upstairs
with a tray of tea and creep into bed with me
and we prop ourselves on elbows and look at each other
and sometimes we talk about love.

TALKING TO JOHN
after you died the silence came

                    which was seemly   which was fitting

people mourn   stand aloof apart

                    gaps between them where distance grows

and white light fills   separates us

                    our few words shadows in the air

we are too far away to hear

                    the quiet falls like snow piles up

each day is the same day

the day after you died

we will not leave you behind

and time has come to a stop

the sky has banished all clouds

air resting after great turmoil

in this aftermath   this ending

still as the white flesh of lilies

this silence is less absolute than yours

though I sit at your desk waiting for you to speak

FALLING IN LOVE WITH THE AA MAN (AND HOW HE TAUGHT ME TO LOVE MY CAR)

Treat her like a friend, said one of the Sons of Morning
leaping from his useful crammed van

in a landscape flat as soup in a grey dish
twilight the A15 North Lincolnshire,

found nothing wrong with my stalled and silent car
and said that she – not *it* but *she* – knew I had plans

to change the car and was *upset, understandably.*
I should be more careful of the car's feelings

and has she got a name? I didn't like to mention
my plan to call it 'Catsmeat Potter Pirbright'

Oh yes, I lied, *her name is Daffodil*
my first and only yellow car – it matched his coat.

So many of them, so many different places:
the back-end of Wembley when I followed a bus

after a Pet Shop Boys gig and got a flat tyre
which a gentle AA giant changed in twelve minutes;

the M62 at midnight one cold November
with passing headlights flashing and drivers hooting

and that heart-melting yellow, hyperreal in the dark –
how he hoisted my third car Pomegranate

onto the back of his lorry, gave me a Twix bar and coffee
and drove us both east over the mountains to Hull,

the old textile towns glinting below and a sour thin moon.
You must love your car he said and so I always have.

Stolid like Barney McGrew and radiant as Blake's Urizen
the sun should always rise behind them pink as fingers –

those men who showed me how to love my cars,
Daffodil, Terracotta, Pomegranate, Russet and good old Red.

But oh my Rosebud, my Sancho Panza, my little Renault 5
comrade, companion, friend for when the going was good –

leaving the Oxford Road at dawn to breakfast among fountains
dodging the lorries overturned like children's toys on Shap,

together we saw that UFO on a May evening over Rydal
together we crawled round Snake Pass, over Snowdonia.

Dear Rosebud you broke down only outside country pubs
until the day your engine fell out and we coasted down

to what was the end of the road for you, and the AA man
broke it to me in a kindly way. They are all kindly men

especially the one who found my old cat Roger
but that is another story.

After You Died: Reading Carole Coates's *When the Swimming Pool Fell into the Sea.*

Many poems in Coates's collection focus on her husband's dementia and eventual death, most notably those at the beginning of the book like the long sequence 'Crazy Days'. I've included 'Crazy Days 1' as an example: it sets up the sequence, detailing how she and her husband were forced to sleep apart after he became delusional, believing he'd discovered a huge hole in their bed. I admire the measured way she recalls the first bed they shared together, kneeling on it to watch him through the bedroom window, too respectful of etiquette to pick fruit from a tree in the garden, 'because you always kept all the rules/as if it would help, as if it would do you good' [4]. The poem implies that tragedy strikes regardless of one's respect for rules; of course it may be that her husband's manners and consideration did him *some* good, given that her fond memory of it closes the 'chasm' between past and present. Yet there's something slightly critical in her assessment of his adherence to rules, and a hint that they've been self-serving ('as if it would do you good'). It's an important qualification, indicative of the tone of the collection: while it registers deep affection for a lost spouse, there's no mawkish idealising, and she depicts their relationship as a very human one, with enough reality and emotional complexity to make us trust her account. It ends on an optimistic note, with a shift to the present tense, but this is qualified too, perhaps, with the word 'sometimes' in the line 'sometimes we talk about love'. Here, as elsewhere in the book, there's a degree of balance and restraint about the way Coates deals with trauma that impresses me.

'Crazy Days 1' is a lovely poem on its own terms, but it feeds into a sequence that gains more power as it progresses. Those who read the entire book will find that in 'Crazy Days 3' her husband retreats into his own head, in 'Crazy Days 4' he thinks she's his mother, in '5' he's caught in a perpetual present, shouting '*Look, Carole, look*' incessantly at the same news story: 'Our circular numb life/is just – again – and then again – and then again – again' [8]. By 'Crazy Days 11', her husband is ostensibly 'cured' – 'The antibodies that attacked your brain/have been repelled' [15] – but in reality he's irretrievably lost: 'those creatures your body loosed on you/have eaten away at both our lives'; her so-called 'cured' husband won't look at photographs of their past, and, even for her, memories have become 'merely a small fragment of living'. Their cherished past is diminished by the ruined present, and the question is whether love can survive such transformations.

Our appreciation of her predicament deepens as we move through the 'Crazy Days' sequence, then, and this continues as we work through the book as a whole. After 'Crazy Days', the poems that deal with her husband's death are particularly affecting. The silence is palpable, for instance, in 'Talking to John', which I've quoted in full here. The powerful opening of this poem strikes with even more force when encountered in the wake of 'Crazy Days': the 'silence' she refers to seems to be part shock, part sadness, and part etiquette for the speaker,[48] and the weight of that silence grows as the poem continues, closing with the line, 'though I sit at your desk waiting for you to speak'. Transient silence is one thing, but the prospect of perpetual silence is another, and by the end of the poem we can identify with the profundity of the loss that the silence signifies. It's thrown into relief by the sense of turmoil in the poems that precede it too, of course, but only those who read the whole collection will appreciate this.

Many poems in the final third of the book don't address the central theme of death directly, but even those not obviously about bereavement are given emotional weight by the earlier sections: we read the later poems in the light of the trauma and sadness she delineates so brilliantly in the opening two thirds, and they're more meaningful and impactful as a result. A good example of this is 'Falling in Love With the AA Man (And How He Taught Me To Love My Car)'. It tells of the dependable AA men who've helped her over the years, 'Stolid like Barney McGrew and radiant as Blake's Urizen'; such men taught her to treat her cars 'like a friend', and to name and humanise them: '*You must love your car* he said and so I always have', naming them all from that point on: like 'Rosebud' her 'little Renault 5/comrade, companion, friend' [63/4]. It is wonderful as a stand-alone poem, but the experience of reading it

---

[48] It's akin perhaps to the American poet Emily Dickinson's 'formal feeling' – the so-called 'Hour of Lead' that comes 'After great pain' [See Emily Dickinson, 'After Great Pain' (poem 341) in *Collected Poems*, Thomas H. Johnson (ed) (London: Faber and Faber, 1975), 162

where it belongs – in her slim volume – is quite different. In the book we view it through the lens of her bereavement, and all that it's taught her about the connections we make with the world outside ourselves. When we read the poem figuratively, it becomes a lesson about love, humanity, and memory: in order to love something we humanise it, and when it breaks down, as cars and people do, those human connections endure at the emotional level. We must cultivate, cherish, and, above all, remember them, and Carole Coates's book can help teach us how – particularly if we read the whole thing.

This is a collection about an ending, of course, except insofar as tragedy gives birth to art. Coates's slim volume was born of suffering, but it might conversely be seen as creatively enriching: the poet-artist survived the ordeal of loss, was altered and diminished by it, but emerged with experience that informed her creative life. As Anaïs Nin said, 'great art was born of great terrors, great loneliness, great inhibitions, instabilities, and it always balances them'[49]. Such combinations of mourning and consolation are typical of elegy as a genre, and one of its social and psychological functions.[50] Along with other things, Coates's book reminds us of how we can use art, not just to explore, but to offset suffering: inspiration and consolation.

How Can Poets Use It?

- Earlier we saw how Roy McFarlane addressed strong emotion by making it explicit, and in this respect his tone

---

[49] Anaïs Nin, *Diary of Anaïs Nin, 1944-1947*, Gunther Stuhlmann (ed), (Swallow Press, 1966), 65

was very different to Coates – his linguistic excesses and adjective-laden flourishes reflect an aesthetic that always seems to teeter on the edge of sentimentality. By contrast Coates is more restrained, and she seems to manage a degree of detachment from her trauma. This is the approach that we associate more with high art, where sentimentality is generally seen as something to be avoided. Poets can learn a lot from Coates's treatment of bereavement, particularly from the clever way she focuses on memories that reveal aspects of the experience, like the episode with the bed in 'Crazy Days 1', or sitting silent at her husband's desk in 'Talking to John'. She makes such incidents speak for the emotion, which is generally a more effective way of engaging readers with it. In the final lines of 'Talking to John', for instance, we feel we are with her, waiting for her late husband to speak, acutely conscious of the absence that drives the poem.

• Coates is very good at pacing her poems. Her lines exude composure and patience; notice how her long lines sometimes contribute to this, together with her thoughtful formatting: she slows down the pace of 'Talking to John' with her dropped lines, for instance, and her use of long white spaces within those lines could be said to visually represent silence on the page.

---

[50] For a discussion of elegy and the conflict between 'consolation and desolation' see Toshiaki Komura's *Poetry of Lost Loss: A Study of the Modern Anti-Consolatory Elegy* (Proquest Publishing, 2011); for a discussion of the function and enduring nature of the 'consolation' elegy see Diana Fuss, *Dying Modern: A Meditation on Elegy* (Duke University Press, 2013)

Writing Prompts

• Think of a traumatic moment in your life and identify a single image that you associate with it. Write a poem that uses that image as a starting point.

• Reread 'Talking to John' and write a poem that imagines the sudden absence of someone you love. Consider their absence in relation to the subsequent silence in your life – for instance, how might that silence be experienced, and at what time of day would it be felt the most?

• Reread 'Falling in Love With the AA Man'. Write a poem that anthropomorphises something that you don't ordinarily think about too much, but which you feel might be underappreciated – such as a cash point machine, or the roof of your house. What is the effect of humanising it, and what emotions does it conjure?

Slim Volumes in a Similar Vein

If you enjoy this collection you might also try *When All the World Is Old* by John Rybicki (Lookout Books, 2012), *Museum Pieces* by Wendy Pratt (Prolebooks, 2013), *To the Boneyard* by Barbara Marsh (Eyewear, 2013), *The Stone Messenger* by Eileen Carney Hulme (Indigo Dreams, 2015), *Downpour* by Ruth Valentine (Smokestack, 2016), *Yours, etcetera* by R.V Bailey (Indigo Dreams, 2019), *The Last Parent* by Anne Stewart (Second Light Publications, 2019), *The Unmapped Woman* by Abegail Morley (Nine Arches Press, 2020), and, on the issue of dementia, *Touch My Head Softly* by Eileen P. Kennedy (Finishing Line Press, 2021).

Sean Elliott's *Poems: 1998-2016*[51]

WE STUDY KINDNESS

Ambitious of a certain fame
I wanted twenty years of work:
the time to make a modest name,
to win a minor kind of prize,
a steady burning of the wick.
The gods willed otherwise.

I'll meet my death in middle age,
no old man's fainting into night,
a sorting out of mortgages
and drugs before the last surprise,
much spitting but no noble fight;
the gods willed otherwise.

The worst is reaching fifty-one
and noticing how much I love
my stubborn wife. What can be done?
We study kindness; I devise
plans for us we'll never prove,
the gods will otherwise.

THE FOOTBALL STAND

'What if I am?' The numbness round my lips,
her voice now timorous, the football pitch
beyond the varnished benches trampled mud;

---

[51] Sean Elliott, *Poems: 1998-2016* (London: Greenwich Exchange Publishing, 2020). All quotations will be taken from this edition.

ridiculous, our dreams now in eclipse,
college and career lost in one quick switch,
I held her hand, felt drained of breath and blood.

A false alarm: not that I guessed it when
we sheltered there for three hours after school,
then nowhere for us but our parents and

the gossip of their working days. What men
have loved her since and was I just a fool,
planning our future on that rain-drenched stand?

GOAT SONG

What better than those gentle afternoons,
learning a lover's most important lesson?
Patient to tease, to lap, to stop or press on,
caught in the urgency of *now* or *soon* ...

until I rode your tide, still kissing as
your heel cupped round my skull or pushed me back
and so we'd rest before love's next attack,
a blameless way to let a summer pass.

Back then I was an ignorant young goat
learning to find my joy in pleasing you;
twenty years on, it's curious to note
our pastimes may have caused my cancered throat:
a nobler cause than cigarettes, it's true,
but quite a footnote on the verb 'to screw'.

The Gods Willed Otherwise: Reading Sean Elliott's *Poems: 1998-2016*

Sean Elliott, was born in Dawlish in 1965 and died prematurely from cancer in 2016. He published poems in numerous journals throughout his life, and Greenwich Exchange released his collected works, *Poems: 1998-2016*, shortly after his death. It includes the final poem he wrote, 'We Study Kindness'. This poem appears near the end of the book, and by the time we reach it we can't help wishing Elliott had been *more* 'Ambitious of a certain kind of fame': perhaps then we'd be holding a thicker volume in our hands. He had the talent to achieve more than a 'modest' name, but modesty seems to define the character we sense behind this poem, and most of his work: it's discernible in his style, and it's one of the reasons we trust his voice. His modesty is more than mere self-deprecation – it's indicative of a certain type of honesty, reflecting what B.J. Sokol says of him in the book's introduction, 'Sean's personal demeanor reflected no egotistical tendencies at all' [14].

That Elliott appears to have no interest in distortion or self-deceit is part of his appeal, and key to his aesthetic. He explains the latter in his 'Art Lessons' sequence, specifically 'In Defence of Realism', where he celebrates the virtues of being true to the world. There isn't space here to include it in full, but the final stanza reads:

> Easy to deride such a scrupulous
> approach as unimaginative, drained
> of deeper meaning, as another craze
> for literalness but any lover knows
> this joy in such particulars. It rained,
> the picnic party left, their promise stays. [79]

Being true to life means more than mere documentary verisimilitude for Elliott; it's also about emotional truth: artistic integrity is a little like a lover's promise – the rain might disrupt the promised picnic party, but as long as the promise is authentic, that at least can't be diminished or corrupted. It's the commitment to truth that 'stays', and hence it's that commitment that matters.

Elliott's tone, themes and sensibility as a poet are eminently compatible with traditional forms, and almost all of his work employs metrical verse: the constraints seem to augment rather than compromise our sense of his authenticity, which is a sure sign of a genuine craftsman. One good example, 'The Football Stand', is about a moment when his life could have changed forever, were his girlfriend's pregnancy not a 'false alarm' [22]. This feels very much like a lived experience. One theme here is the folly of making plans, but notice how the idea of life's unpredictability is countered by the poem's form, with its regularity of stresses and rhyme asserting the very predictability that reality denies us. I can't help seeing traditional poetic form as a parallel for tradition in a broader sense in this poem. For instance, does it represent the convention of marriage that he was prepared to accept when he thought he had to? I'm not sure if this is what Elliott has in mind, but the metrical beat seems to complement the theme in a delightfully subtle and suggestive way, as is often the case in his work.

As with Butt and Etty, humour is part of Elliott's aesthetic, and I think this helps him keep emotions in check when he needs to, offering a useful corrective to sentimentality and self-pity. A good example is 'Goat Song', which concerns his suspicion that having oral sex with his wife contributed to the mouth cancer that finally killed him. It's hard to think of a less self-pitying poem, and I love the final line, 'but quite a footnote on the verb "to screw"' [134]. The double meaning of the phrase 'to screw' is funny, of course, and indicative of the attitude to life suggested in many of his poems. Where metre and rhyme can suggest inevitability, it can also suggest acceptance, as I think it does here: the tone is sanguine as the poem builds inexorably to a couplet that acknowledges the speaker's sealed fate. In 'The Football Stand' and 'We Study Kindness' he reminds us that the future isn't foreseeable, and 'Goat Song' confirms it, but the tone and rhythm imply a speaker who is reconciled to the fact that 'the gods willed otherwise', and who senses that there's little to do but laugh about it. Thus in a poem about death he teaches us something about life.

This all-too-slim slim volume presents a poet's entire oeuvre, and there's no doubt it gains power and poignancy from our knowledge of his early death: like the Coates collection, and indeed all the books here, we must read the entire thing to benefit fully, as the knowledge we gain from some poems impacts on the way we read others. The poems are augmented by their context – not least our developing understanding of the creative presence behind them: his humour, his authenticity, and his modesty, all signify more strongly as we encounter it in poem after poem, compounded by the reality of the tragedy that followed. Perhaps Elliott, and poets like him, give us a frame within which to read *all* poems: as statements against death. 'This,' as Miroslav Hulub suggests, 'is one sense of poetry. A little concoction of words against death. It's almost the instinct against death crystallised'.[52]

How Can Poets Use It?

• As with Orem, Elliott has a fondness for traditional verse, and he writes it with a fluency that is hard to achieve without a lot of practice. His verse never feels strained or contrived. Reading Elliott offers an insight into what can be achieved with formal verse, and its contemporary relevance. With so many poets favouring free verse in the modern world, traditional verse can sometimes feel démodé, but that's never the case with Elliot. Importantly he doesn't offer elaborate displays of technical virtuosity; rather he creates deceptively simple, unpretentious verse that effortlessly reinforces his themes. He is an excellent model for writers whose talents suit this style of expression.

• Elliott's use of rhyme and metre is never at odds with his insistence on authenticity, and his adherence to the latter provides his most useful lesson for poets. As with Robert Etty, his best poems have a sense of directness and veracity that cannot be achieved via rhetorical tricks: it begins with a commitment to reality that demands courage, but also humility. It sometimes means finding ways of circumventing the ego, but above all it depends on a willingness to deal honestly with emotions. One obvious step towards achieving this in poems is to avoid the natural inclination many of us have to evade issues, or to idealise other people, or, more importantly, ourselves.

---

[52] Dennis O'Driscoll (ed), *The Bloodaxe Book of Poetry Quotations* (Bloodaxe, 2006), 238

Writing Prompts

• Reread 'The Football Stand'. Think of a moment when your life could have been changed forever: the job you didn't get, for instance, or the relationship that didn't work out. Focus on the details of the incident itself and its status as a potentially pivotal moment in your life.

• Write a poem about unpredictability or chaos that employs regular rhyme and metre. Try to personalise it, referring to a specific moment when you became aware of contingency in your own life: it doesn't matter whether the disruptions were merely threatened or fully realised, the important thing is to explore the tension between instability and the perceived order of traditional metrical form.

Slim Volumes in a Similar Vein

If you are drawn to the themes of Elliot's book you might also like *Close Reading* by Floyd Skloot (Eyewear, 2016), *The Fetch* by Gregory Leadbetter (Nine Arches Press, 2016), *The Year of the Crab* by Gordon Meade (Cultured Llama, 2018), and *The End* by Gareth Writer-Davies (Arenig Press, 2019). If you warm to the style of his verse you might also enjoy *An Almost Dancer: Poems 2005-2011* by Robert Nye (Greenwich Exchange, 2012), David Sutton, *No Through Road* (Greenwich Exchange, 2013), and Michael W. Thomas, *Under Smoky Light* (Offa's Press, 2020).

CONCLUSION: USE BOOKS

'Nothing overtly significant needs to be happening in a poem. The doors of perception need be no bigger than a speck of dust, but when any one of them opens it is as if the whole of life were swirling behind it.'

– George Szirtes[53]

It may seem as if the internet has 'the whole of life [...] swirling behind it', but our level of engagement with that 'life' is mostly superficial, and persistently undermined by the myriad of distractions that accompany the online experience. Our smartphones use such distractions to keep us hooked for the principal purpose of selling us things, and our creative lives deserve more; the most effective way of becoming the best poets we can be is to *find* more. We can find it in the books I've discussed here. Slim volumes represent the opposite of the smartphone experience. They demand and reward focus and sustained intellectual engagement; they offer depth, encourage critical reflection and creative interplay; they are the 'doors of perception' which, once opened, offer infinitely more profound and meaningful encounters with life. Poets should seek them out because there is no better way of improving your poetry than to read as many slim volumes as possible. I urge poets to put down their phones and luxuriate in slim volumes instead. Hopefully my book has shown ways in which we can read such books as poets, attentive to their cultural relevance, and also to their potential to inspire and instruct us on our own

[53] Dennis O'Driscoll (ed), *The Bloodaxe Book of Poetry Quotations* (Bloodaxe, 2006), 29

creative journey. Don't pick up the phone again until you've read all the books I've mentioned here, then you can phone me to thank me.

The Poet's Bookshelf

How To Books

Jo Bell, *52: Write a Poem a Week: Start Now, Keep Going* (Nine Arches Press, 2015)

This offers a series of 52 prompts designed to inspire poets to write a poem per week. The book includes a variety of writing challenges from poets like Philip Gross, Helen Mort and Luke Kennard, focusing on a different theme each week; it also provides a sample poem on each theme by everyone from Keats to Carol Ann Duffy. It's an innovative approach to the teaching of writing skills, presented in an unpretentious and witty way.

Jo Bell and Jane Commane, *How to be a Poet* (Nine Arches Press, 2017)

A practical guide on how to become a poet by two fine poets. Jane Commane is the editor of Nine Arches Press, as well as the co-editor of the influential *Under the Radar* magazine, and has excellent advice on developing manuscripts for submission. There are useful contributions from other writers too, including both performance and page poets, and throughout the approach is breezy and informal.

W.N. Herbert, *Writing Poetry* (Routledge, 2010)

Much of the material in this book originally formed part of an Open University creative writing course, and it has a rather formal and pedagogical feel in places. However, it presents clear and informed advice on 'seven aspects of contemporary poetry': drafting, line, voice, imagery, rhyme, form and theme. It also includes some good writing exercises, and relevant interviews with contemporary poets such as Douglas Dunn and Kathleeen Jamie.

Amorak Huey and W. Todd Kaneko (ed), *Poetry: A Writers' Guide and Anthology* (Bloomsbury, 2018)

This is another very practical and usable textbook designed for teachers and students of poetry which includes a selection of contemporary poems. The latter range across a variety of forms, all of which are discussed in an accessible text which includes contributions from the poets themselves. The book explains key concepts, and provides an appendix of 'Poetry Experiments' that poets can try in order to develop their craft.

Richard Hugo, *The Triggering Town: Lectures and Essays on Poetry and Writing* (W.W. Norton, 1979).

This book collects some of the essays that the poet Richard Hugo wrote through the course of his career, and together they offer an insightful and entertaining account of the art of poetry. The title essay in particular is worth reading for the excellent distinction made between the subject that 'triggers' a poem, and the 'generated' subject, which might be very different. Hugo has a very witty and accessible style, and this succinct collection is highly regarded among poets and teachers.

Steve Kowit, *In the Palm of Your Hand: The Poet's Portable Workshop* (Tilbury House Publishers, 2019)

Now in a second edition this book takes a 'workshop' approach to learning the craft of poetry, exploring themes such as the poetry of love, desire, loss, and the natural world. It also has sections on technique, including chapters on traditional forms alongside more experimental approaches, such as automatic writing and 'ecstatic poetics'.

Adrian May, *The Magic of Writing* (Macmillan Palgrave, 2018)

My usual advice to poets, in keeping with the theme of my own book, is to read as much as possible, but of course writing also requires inspiration and imagination, which is less easy to define and discuss. This is one of the more interesting and inventive books on the topic, which draws parallels between creative thinking and magic. It presents an informed and convincing account of this idea, together with exercises designed to stimulate creativity. It's more about inspiration than craft, but some poets will find it useful.

Glyn Maxwell, *On Poetry* (Oberon Masters Series, 2012)

One of the sharpest books about poetry from a leading practitioner: Maxwell unpacks his theory of poetry across seven chapters, each taking a theme central to his idea of what poetry is and how it works. He discusses key issues with a group of imaginary creative writing students, having them share their ideas for the benefit of the reader. There's much humour in the book, but Maxwell never loses sight of his purpose: to communicate his personal views on poetry as forcefully as possible.

Nigel McLoughlin (ed), *The Portable Poetry Workshop* (Macmillan Palgrave, 2017)

This offers a series of short essays on a variety of germane topics, all from a practice-based point of view. It covers formal and free verse, and includes many useful exercises. It contains things you might not find elsewhere, such as useful pieces on subjects like riddles in poetry, sprung rhythm, poetry and grammar, and the meaning of meaning.

Mary Oliver, *A Poetry Handbook: A Prose Guide to Understanding and Writing Poetry* (HMH Books, 1994)

This is a succinct book about the craft of writing, very much to the point. A poet of international renown, Oliver writes convincingly about why it's important to study form, but also offers good advice on writing free verse. She has sections on lineation, cadence, imagery, diction, tone, and voice, together with useful advice on reading poetry aloud, and editing one's own work.

Matthew Sweeney and John Hartley Williams, *Write Poetry and Get It Published* (Hodder Education, 2010)

Originally published as part of the 'Teach Yourself' series, this guide to writing poetry is one of the liveliest, least pretentious, and most useful books for beginners. Written with flair and wit, it ranges across a host of relevant topics, and includes numerous imaginative writing exercises: a practical, no-nonsense approach to becoming a poet that has gone through three editions.

General Books About Poetry

Simon Armitage, *A Vertical Art: Oxford Lectures* (Faber and Faber, 2021)

This collects the lectures Armitage gave during his tenure as Oxford University Professor of Poetry. It includes insightful explorations of topics such as the difference between poems and song lyrics, the value of imagery, the idea of the professional poet, and poets in education. He closes with a 'CODA: Ninety-Five Theses: On the Principles and Practice of Poetry' which every poet should read.

John Burnside, *The Music of Time: Poetry in The Twentieth Century* (Profile Books, 2019)

This is an informed study of the themes and preoccupations of twentieth-century poetry which doesn't restrict itself to the Western canon. It's a comprehensive, scholarly book about the socio-cultural relevance of poetry that will deepen anyone's understanding of the art and the foundations of modern verse.

Tom Chivers (ed), *Stress Fractures: Essays on Poetry* (Penned in the Margins Press, 2010)

This is an unusual but interesting collection of essays on poetry that covers a variety of themes. It has an eclectic and non-conventional feel with occasionally quirky takes on topics such as Emily Dickinson, and computer-generated poetry. There are good, thoughtful essays on issues like prose poetry, self-consciousness in poetry, and slam poetry, and I particularly recommend Katy Evan-Bush's excellent piece on lineation, 'The Line'.

Robert Crawford, Henry Hart, David Kinloch, and Richard Price (eds), *Talking Verse: Interviews with the Poets* (Verse, 1996)

This collection of interviews won't be familiar to everyone, but it is well worth seeking out. It was published by the University of St Andrews in the mid-nineties, and includes many interesting pieces from some high profile poets of the late twentieth century.

Jonathan Davidson, *On Poetry* (Smith/Doorstop Books, 2018)

This is a series of short essays and autobiographical pieces that address the author's lifelong love of poetry. He discusses the poems that have meant a lot to him during his life, offering perceptive analyses of numerous poems. As a longtime director of Writing West Midlands, and an excellent poet in his own right, Davidson's insights are both culturally informed and illuminating. He expands many of the themes in a later book, *A Commonplace* (Smith/Doorstop Books, 2020), where he juxtaposes his own poems with poems that have inspired him, contextualising both for the benefit of the reader. Together the two books offer a unique account of a poet's creative life, and I recommend them both.

Michael Donaghy, *The Shape of the Dance: Essays, Interviews and Digressions* (Picador, 2009)

A very readable collection of writings from a superb poet, published as a companion volume to his posthumous *Collected Poems*. Donaghy was a champion of cadence in verse, and he writes very well about poetry and form. The stand-out piece is 'Wallflowers: A Lecture on Poetry with Misplaced Notes and Additional Heckling' in which he talks about the relationship between poets and readers with imaginative and apposite references to dance. He was an astute critic of other people's work, and he writes very well about a range of poets, including T.S. Eliot, John Updike, and Elizabeth Bishop.

Eric Falci, *The Value of Poetry* (Cambridge University Press, 2020)

Despite W.H. Auden's contention that 'poetry makes nothing happen', scholars often value poetry for its ability to challenge the dominant ideology, offering ways of interrogating and undermining the cultural/political status quo. While this doesn't really feature in my notion of poetry's value in *Don't Use the Phone*, readers can find an excellent discussion of such ideas in this book.

Donald Hall, *Breakfast Served Any Time of Day: Essays on Poetry New and Selected* (University of Michigan Press, 2003)

This is a selection of essays from the former US Poet Laureate and distinguished critic, Donald Hall. It begins with an enjoyable piece called 'The Unsayable Said' which attempts to introduce poetry to sceptical readers, and includes essays addressed to young poets, offering sage advice on subjects like dead metaphor, theory, ambition, and a host of other relevant subjects.

W.N. Herbert and Matthew Hollis (eds), *Strong Words: Modern Poets On Poetry* (Bloodaxe, 2000)

This is a collection of manifestos on poetry from some of the most important poets of the twentieth century, from Auden to William Carlos Williams. It also includes commissioned pieces from over 30 more contemporary practitioners, making it a very useful book of wisdom, although an updated edition would be welcome.

Ben Lerner, *The Hatred of Poetry* (Fitzcarraldo Editions, 2016)

This is an extended essay that uses the idea of a hatred of poetry as a springboard into a discussion of its function and cultural value. Beginning with Plato, Lerner explores the reasons why poetry is often disparaged, and why we seem to have a love/hate relationship with it. He offers a cogent case for its importance, and his account includes some illuminating readings of, among others, Walt Whitman and Emily Dickinson. It is a worthwhile book for those who want to develop their sense of what poetry means. While some say that it's more of a book for critics than poets, I don't think there's a distinction between the two.

Craig Raine, *My Grandmother's Glasseye: A Look At Poetry* (Atlantic Books, 2016)

A witty and often opinionated book on poetry from the former Poetry Editor at Faber & Faber. He focuses on how poetry works, offering entertaining chapters on subjects like definition, vagueness, rhythm, line, metaphor, and sub-text. He champions 'common sense' and 'clarity' in his approach to poetry, and seeks to demystify the form. Raine spends a lot of time attacking other critics, and his tone can be a little cantankerous, but he offers thorough and convincing readings of many poems, and his book is entertaining throughout.

Mary Ruefle, *Madness, Rack, and Honey: Collected Lectures* (Wave Books, 2012)

A very readable book which collects a series of lectures from the American poet and professor, Mary Ruefle. She discusses topics such as beginnings, sentimentality, and theme, illustrating her points with critically astute references to a wide range of poets. She is a very entertaining writer, who expresses herself with clarity and verve, and while her comments are occasionally a little eccentric, they are always stimulating.

Vijay Seshadri, *Poets At Work: Interviews from the Paris Review* (Paris Review Editions, 2021)

This chunky volume collects some of the notable interviews with poets conducted over its seventy-year history, including interviews with Yehuda Amichai, John Ashbery, Frank Bidart, Elizabeth Bishop, Allen Ginsberg, Susan Howe, Robert Lowell, Marianne Moore, Pablo Neruda, Ezra Pound, Ishmael Reed, Mark Strand, Derek Walcott. This book is a special edition published by *The Paris Review*, but see also an earlier *Poets at Work*, edited by George Plimpton, with an introduction by Donald Hall (Penguin, 1989).

David Wheatley, *Contemporary British Poetry* (Macmillan Palgrave, 2015)

This is a book for those looking to understand the cultural context of contemporary poetry and learn about the critical debates around subjects such as postcolonialism, gender, class, and the environment. It focuses on the work of high-profile critics like Christopher Ricks and Geoffery Hill, and has good sections on prize culture in the UK, and the making of the canon.

The Presses

The seventeen slim volumes I've chosen to discuss all come from small independent presses. I've listed them below, and I urge poets to explore their other publications.

Cinnamon Press

Cinnamon Press is a family-run press based in North Wales, who until 2020 published the long-running *Envoi* poetry journal. They pride themselves on not being 'defined by genre' and seek to publish 'thought provoking' and 'innovative' work. In my view they succeed, and as well as poetry their list includes wonderful novels and short story collections. Cinnamon authors have won and been shortlisted for numerous prizes, including Wales Book of the Year, The Saboteur Awards, and Not the Booker Prize.
https://www.cinnamonpress.com/index.php

Doire Press

Doire Press is one of Ireland's most prestigious small presses. Founded in 2007 in Connemara by Lisa Frank and John Walsh, it publishes 'new and emerging writers who give voice to what it means to be Irish in a changing Ireland'. Its books have won and been shortlisted for several awards, including the Edge Hill Readers' Prize, Shine/Strong Award, EU Prize for Literature, and the Forward Prize. It is supported by the Arts Council of Ireland and the Arts Council of Northern Ireland.
https://www.doirepress.com/about

Greenwich Exchange Publishing

Founded in 1988, Greenwich Exchange is a small, independent literary house publishing a wide range of quality material, including biography, criticism, fiction, philosophy, and poetry. Their poetry list is pleasingly eclectic, and includes world-class work from established and emerging writers.
https://greenex.co.uk/

Hazel Press

Hazel Press is a newly-established publisher with a particular interest in the environment, climate change, and feminism. They aim to publish work that 'engages with a strong sense of place and the important ecological issues of our time'. Hazel Press produce delightful chapbooks, and their notable recent publications include Matthew Hollis's *Leaves*, and Ella Duffy's innovative sequence, *Rootstalk*, both released in 2020.
https://hazelpress.co.uk/

Iron Press

Iron Press ploughs its own furrow as other 'publishers become more corporate, global and boring'. It began as the publisher of *Iron Magazine* in 1973, a respected literary journal that ran for 26 years; the press survives as an occasional publisher of 'new quality writing', under the careful editorship of Peter Mortimer.
https://www.ironpress.co.uk/

Nine Arches Press

Nine Arches Press was founded in 2008 when it began publishing the highly-regarded *Under the Radar* magazine. Nine Arches soon introduced chapbooks and full-length collections to their output, and by the end of the noughties had a strong list that included prose fiction. Since then they have developed into a leading independent publisher, and their books have won and been shortlisted for many prizes, including the East Midlands Book Award, Michael Marks Poetry Pamphlet Prize, and the T.S. Eliot Poetry Prize

https://ninearchespress.com/

Shoestring Press

Shoestring operates out of Beeston, Nottingham, and was created by the poet and academic John Lucas. John developed skills as a publisher by helping to run Reading University Press as a postgraduate, and created The Byron Press when he moved to Nottingham in the 60s, which survived for a decade. He began Shoestring in 1994, which continues to thrive with a superb list that includes poetry, fiction and memoir.

http://www.shoestringpress.co.uk/

Smokestack Books

Smokestack is an independent publisher of 'radical and unconventional' poetry run by the distinguished poet Andy Croft. Shortlisted for the British Book Awards Small Press of the Year in 2019 and 2020, it has a comprehensive list that includes high profile writers like John Berger, Ian McMillan, and Michael Rosen, among a wealth of lesser-known talents. Its list of international poetry is particularly impressive.

https://smokestack-books.co.uk/

Wheelbarrow Books

Wheelbarrow Books is an imprint of the Residential College in the Arts and Humanities Center for Poetry, and printed by the Michigan State University in the US; they publish two new volumes of poetry annually, which are the winners of the Wheelbarrow Books Poetry Prize (awarded to authors yet to publish a collection of original poetry).

https://poetry.rcah.msu.edu/wheelbarrow-books/index.html

Acknowledgements

Some portions of this book were developed from reviews/articles written for a variety of journals, and thanks are due to: *Envoi, High Windows, The Lake, London Grip, Poetry Quarterly Review*, and *Poetry Salzburg Review*. I discovered some of the books I mention in my role as a judge for the Rubery Book Award, and I'd like to thank the Rubery Prize Director, Heather Morrall, and the judges I've worked with over the years: Clare Morrall, Kerry Hadley-Pryce, Narinder Dhami, Judith Allnatt, and Pauline Morgan. I'd like to thank all of the publishers of the books I've discussed, of course, and the writers. All concerned gave permission for me to quote from their publications free of charge. Special thanks are due to James Hodgson, John Lucas, and Andy Croft for their help and advice.

The Author

Paul McDonald taught at the University of Wolverhampton for twenty-five years, where he ran the Creative Writing Programme. He took early retirement in 2019 to write full time. He is the author of over twenty books, covering fiction, poetry, and scholarship. His creative work has won and been shortlisted for numerous prizes including The Artlyst Art to Poetry Award, The Bedford Prize, The Bridport Prize, The John Clare Poetry Prize, the Liverpool Poetry Prize, the Ottakars/Faber and Faber Poetry Competition, the Pushcart Prize (nomination), the Sentinel Poetry Prize, the Sentinel Short Story Prize, and the Retreat West Flash Fiction Prize.